MUSIC FOR LIVING

In Our Country

Book Five

JAMES L. MURSELL

GLADYS TIPTON

BEATRICE LANDECK

HARRIET NORDHOLM

ROY E. FREEBURG

JACK M. WATSON

Woodcuts by Jean Mursell

CALIFORNIA STATE SERIES

Published by

CALIFORNIA STATE DEPARTMENT OF EDUCATION

Sacramento, 1958

Acknowledgments

Grateful acknowledgment is made to the following for the use of their material. If we have omitted any names, we trust we may be forgiven, as we have made every effort to locate all copyright owners.

American Evangelical Lutheran Youth Fellowship for "Bugle Note" from A WORLD OF SONG, copyright 1941. Used by permission.

Artists and Writers Guild, Inc., for the poem "Open Range" from COWBOYS AND INDIANS, a Giant Golden Book, by Kathryn and Byron Jackson, copyright 1948 by Simon and Schuster, Inc., and Artists and Writers Guild, Inc.

Boosey and Hawkes Inc. for "Eight Bells" from SEA SONGS by Ferris Tozer, reprinted by permission of the copyright owners, Boosey and Hawkes Inc.

The Boy Scouts Association of Great Britain for "We're All Together Again" from the BOY SCOUT SONG BOOK.

Mrs. Wilson Brewer for the poem "Rain Music" by Joseph Cotter, Jr., from THE BAND OF GIDEON, published by The Cornhill Company.

The Carib Singers for "Basay Down."

M. M. Cole Publishing Company for "Wabash Cannon Ball."

Cooperative Recreation Service, Inc., for "The Happy Ploughman," "Pol Perica," and "Calaloo."

Crown Publishers, Inc., for the melodies, "*La Sandunga*" and "Vendor's Song" ("*A Pregon*"), from A TREASURY OF MEXICAN FOLKWAYS by Frances Toor.

Estate of Stella Marek Cushing for "Ah, Lovely Meadows," "Kites Are Flying," and "The Shepherds."

H. L. Davis for the excerpt from his poem "Proud Riders," from PROUD RIDERS, published by Harper & Brothers, 1942.

Dodd, Mead & Company for "In a Sugar Camp" from AMERICAN PRIMITIVE MUSIC by Frederick Burton.

Judith Eisenstein for "Purim Song" from SONGS OF CHILDHOOD by Judith Eisenstein and Frida Prinsky.

Franciscan Fathers of California for "*El Alabado*" from MISSION MUSIC OF CALIFORNIA by the Reverend Owen da Silva, O. F. M.

Robert Gartias for the song, "Teru Teru Bozu."

The H. W. Gray Company, Inc., for "Ground Hog" from LONESOME TUNES, copyright 1916, renewed 1944 by the H. W. Gray Company, Inc. Used by permission.

Harcourt, Brace and Company, Inc., for the poem "Buffalo Dusk" from EARLY MOON by Carl Sandburg, copyright 1920, 1930, by Harcourt, Brace and Company, Inc.; also for "Abalone," "Bigerlow," "Driving Steel" ("Hammer Man"), "I Found a Horseshoe," "The Railroad Cars Are Coming," and "The Little Old Sod Shanty," all from THE AMERICAN SONGBAG by Carl Sandburg.

Harper & Brothers for selections from "The Promise of America" in YOU CAN'T GO HOME AGAIN by Thomas Wolfe, copyright 1940 by Maxwell Perkins as executor, and from "April, Late April" in THE WEB AND THE ROCK by Thomas Wolfe, copyright 1937 by Maxwell Perkins as executor; also for the poem "Wheat Fields" from I SPEND THE SUMMER by James S. Tippett, copyright 1930 by Harper & Brothers.

Ralph Hess for the two Indian songs, "Desert Fruit" ("Strength to Carry the Burden Basket") and "My Corn Seeds."

Burl Ives for "Utah Iron Horse" and "Song of the Fishes" from THE BURL IVES SONG BOOK.

Gladys V. Jameson for "Mingo Mountain" from SWEET FREEDOM'S SONG published by Cooperative Recreation Service Inc.

Ruth C. Koch for a selection from "The Green Bench" from LET US BE MERRY by Agnes Louise Dean.

Eunice M. Lehmer for "Fingers of the Sun" and "Lonely Is the Hogan" from SONGS OF THE MESA by Derrick Norman Lehmer.

Liveright Publishing Corporation for the melody of "Michi Banjo" from PLAYTIME WITH MUSIC by Charity Bailey and Marion Abeson; copyright 1952.

Ruby Terrill Lomax for "Sis Joe" from OUR SINGING COUNTRY and for "Connecticut Peddler" from AMERICAN BALLADS AND FOLK SONGS, both published by The Macmillan Company.

The Macmillan Company for the poem "Swift Things Are Beautiful" from AWAY GOES SALLY by Elizabeth Coatsworth.

Edward B. Marks Music Corporation for "Tic-Ti Tic-Ta," "*Las Mañanitas*," and "Bonita"; also for "*En Roulant Ma Boule*" from SONGS TO GROW ON by Beatrice Landeck. Used by permission of Edward B. Marks Music Corporation, copyright owners.

Marjorie M. Neefe for her translation and adaptation of "Shy Incognita."

Oxford University Press, London, for "Donkey Riding" from THE OXFORD SONG BOOK, VOL. 2, and for the English translation of "The Brook," reprinted from SCHUBERT'S SONGS TRANSLATED by A. Fox Strangways and Steuart Wilson.

University of Pennsylvania Press for "My Sweetheart's the Mule in the Mines" and "Down in a Coal Mine" from MINSTRELS OF THE MINE PATCH by George Korson; also for "Joe Magerac" from PENNSYLVANIA SONGS AND LEGENDS by George Korson.

Theodore Presser Co. for "Zuni Sunset Song" from TRADITIONAL SONGS OF THE ZUNI INDIANS, by Carlos Troyer.

G. Schirmer, Inc., for the melody of "Suzette" from BAYOU BALLADS by Mina Monroe, and for the melody of "My Raincape" ("*El Capotin*") from SONGS OF OLD CALIFORNIA by Charles F. Lummis.

Paul A. Schmitt Music Company for "Little Burro" ("*Charrada*") and "The Lemon Tree" ("*Pajara Pinta*"), from CANCIONITAS by Roberta McLaughlin and Bessie Mae Stanchfield.

Texas Folklore Society for "Don't Let Your Watch Run Down" from SOUTH TEXAS NEGRO WORK SONGS by Gates Thomas.

Janet Tobitt for "Music in the Barn" ("Cissie in the Barn") from PROMENADE ALL; and "Navajo Happy Song," "Sweep the Floor" ("*De Bezem*"), and "Lumberman's Song," all from THE DITTY BAG.

United States Marine Corps for "The Marines' Hymn."

The Viking Press, Inc., for "Choppin" ("He's A-Choppin' in de New Groun'") and "Chimney Sweeper" from ROLLING ALONG IN SONG by Rosamond Johnson, copyright 1937 by The Viking Press, Inc.

The music in this book was reproduced from hand written originals by Maxwell Weaner.

© 1956 SILVER BURDETT COMPANY
International Copyright Secured
All Rights Reserved

printed in
CALIFORNIA STATE PRINTING OFFICE
SACRAMENTO 1ST PRINT, 300M 1958

Our country is a tapestry,
  Woven by loving hands;
By Faith and Hope 'twas deftly made
  From threads of other lands;
And each retains its native hue
  Whose beauty animates
A varied pattern, lovely, new—
  Our own United States.
    —ANNA LOUISE DABNEY

Contents

Land of Many Beauties 1

Early Settlers in Our Land 16
FROM SPAIN . . . FROM FRANCE
FROM OLD ENGLAND TO NEW ENGLAND
OLD ENGLAND TO NEW VIRGINIA
FROM HOLLAND AND GERMANY

Workers Build America 49
GATHERING NATURE'S BOUNTY
HARVESTS AND HERDS

Journeys and Adventurings 86
OPENING UP THE LAND
THE FORTY-NINERS
INTO THE WEST

Our Enduring Memories 121

Lands Beyond the States 145

Many Peoples—One Nation 156
CITY STREETS . . . COUNTRY LANES
FESTIVALS AND DANCES

Round the Calendar 201

More Songs to Sing 217

Indices 225

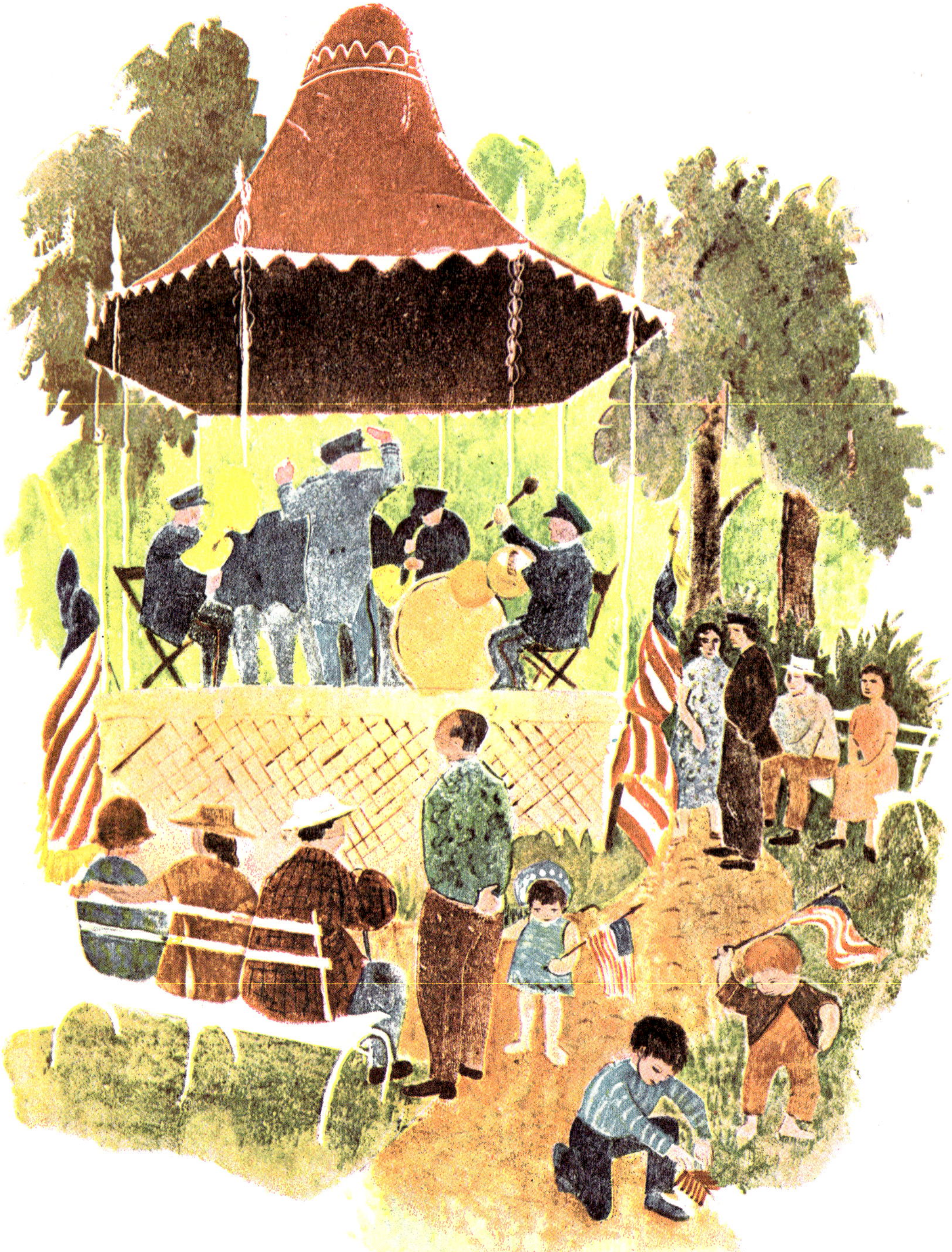

LAND OF MANY BEAUTIES

America the Beautiful

WORDS BY KATHERINE LEE BATES
MUSIC BY SAMUEL WARD

1. O beau - ti - ful for spa - cious skies, For am - ber waves of grain,
2. O beau - ti - ful for pil - grim feet, Whose stern im - pas - sioned stress

For pur - ple moun - tain maj - es - ties A - bove the fruit - ed plain!
A thor - ough - fare for free - dom beat A - cross the wil - der - ness!

A - mer - i - ca! A - mer - i - ca! God shed His grace on thee,
A - mer - i - ca! A - mer - i - ca! God mend thine ev - 'ry flaw,

And crown thy good with broth - er - hood, From sea to shin - ing sea!
Con - firm thy soul in self - con - trol, Thy lib - er - ty in law!

3. O beautiful for heroes proved
　In liberating strife,
　Who more than self
　　their country loved,
　And mercy more than life!
　America! America!
　May God thy gold refine,
　Till all success be nobleness,
　And ev'ry gain divine!

4. O beautiful for patriot dream
　That sees, beyond the years,
　Thine alabaster cities gleam
　Undimmed by human tears!
　America! America!
　God shed His grace on thee,
　And crown thy good
　　with brotherhood,
　From sea to shining sea!

STARTING FROM PAUMANOK

Land of the pastoral plains, the grass-fields of the world!
Land of those sweet-air'd interminable plateaus!
Land of the herd, the garden, the healthy house of adobe!
Lands where the northwest Columbia winds, and where the southwest Colorado winds!
Land of the eastern Chesapeake! Land of the Delaware!
Land of Ontario, Erie, Huron, Michigan!
Land of the Old Thirteen! Massachusetts land! Land of Vermont and Connecticut!
Land of the ocean shores! Land of sierras and peaks!

—WALT WHITMAN

Open Range

WORDS BY KATHRYN AND BYRON JACKSON
MUSIC BY MILTON KAYE

1. Prai-rie goes to the moun-tain, Moun-tain goes to the sky, The sky sweeps a-cross to the dis-tant hills And there, in the mid-dle, Am I.
2. Hills crowd to the riv-er, Riv-er runs by the tree, Tree throws its shad-ow on sun-burnt grass And here, in the shad-ow, Is me.

3. Shadows creep up the mountain,
   Mountain goes black on the sky,
   The sky bursts out with a million stars
   And here, by the campfire, Am I.

The Wide Fields

You will feel like hiking as you sing this 4-H Club song about America's vast prairies.

WORDS BY FANNIE R. BUCHANAN
MUSIC BY RENA M. PARISH

Sing for the wide, wide fields,_____
Sing for the wide, wide sky,_____
Sing for the good, glad earth,_____ For the sun on hill-tops high._____ Sing for the com-rade true,_____ Sing for the friend-ship sweet;_____
Sing as to-geth-er we swing a-long,
With the turf be-neath our feet._____

Copyright 1948, Natl. Committee on Boys and Girls Club Work, Inc., Chicago. Used by permission.

The Brook

TRANSLATED BY A. STRANGWAYS AND S. WILSON
MUSIC BY FRANZ SCHUBERT

A - mong the rocks and heath - er
I heard a ti - ny rill;
It spar - kled in the sun - light
And prat - tled down the hill.
I know not how it drew me, I nev - er ques-tioned why;
We could not choose but fol - low, My trust - y staff and I,
We could not choose but fol - low, My trust - y staff and I.

*Small, loved brooks
make great rivers
that turn the wheels of America,
before finding the sea.*

East, West — Home's Best

WORDS BY ALICE WHITE
CATALONIAN FOLK SONG

1. How I wish that I could be
Where the fresh sea winds are sigh - ing,
Where the tide runs swift and free,
And, a - bove, the sea gulls cry - ing.

2. South Sea islands I have seen,
   Heard the Arctic glacier's thunder,
   Mountain peaks and castles fair,
   All have filled my heart with wonder.

3. Oh, but dearer far to me
   Are the hills in sunset glowing,
   Evenings bright with countless stars,
   In my homeland where I'm going.

Song of the Wind

UTE MOUNTAIN AIR

The Utes, plateau Indians now in Utah, believe the wind carries a song of their ancestors as it blows across the water.

Melody flutes and voices make the wind sounds

Oo ___ Oo ___ Oo ___

Oo ___

On the moun-tain I hear the ___ sound of the

Oo ___

wind; Hear it blow-ing a-cross the ___ deep blue

Oo ___ Oo. ___

wa-ter, Hear it blow-ing on the

Oo. _____ Oo. _____

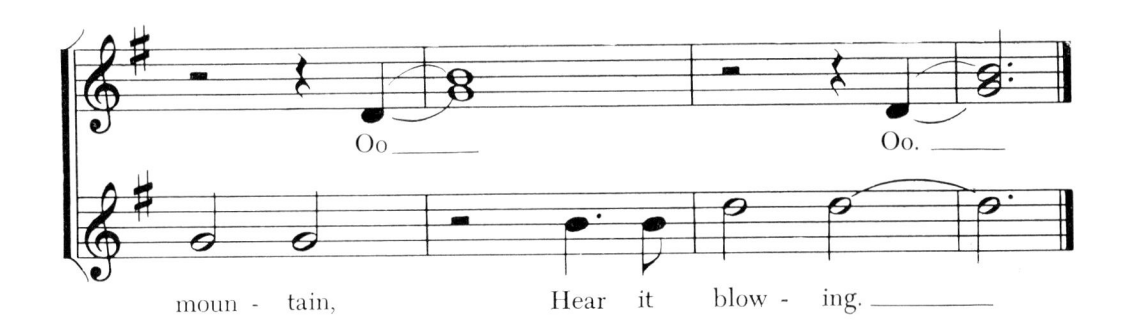

moun - tain, Hear it blow - ing. _____

Bugle Note

GERMAN FOLK SONG

B♭ Trumpets play this introduction

1. The wood - lands sleep in si - lence deep; Not
2. From camp re - mote, a bu - gle note Comes
3. The woods re - peat the ech - oes sweet O'er

e'en a leaf is stirred. _____ Not e'en a leaf is stirred. _____
through the night so still. _____ Comes through the night so still. _____
lake, from glen and hill. _____ O'er lake from glen and hill. _____

The bird's at rest with - in its nest, And not a sound is
And all a - round the ech - oes sound O'er field and for - est
The soft re - frain comes back a - gain And then the night is

heard. _____ And not a sound _____ is heard. _____
hill. _____ O'er field and for - est hill. _____
still. _____ And then the night _____ is still. _____

Desert Fruit

TRANSLATED BY RALPH HESS
PAPAGO INDIAN AIR

O Mountain Spirit, come, Oh, come to me and make me strong, make me strong. Baskets of cactus fruit will I bear. O Spirit of the hills, Oh, stay with me and make me strong, make me strong, Bearing on my shoulders the fruit. Far across the desert I go, Mountain Spirit, stay with me,____ stay with me.

The Papagos are Pima Indians, descendants of an ancient culture that flourished in our southwestern mesa country long before the coming of the white man. They built irrigating canals and had verdant farms where now only cactus fruit grows. Ages of rain and wind have exposed the colored shales and sandstones in the badlands east of the Grand Canyon. This is the Painted Desert, which is studded with curious rock formations, where harder rock resisted erosion by the elements.

Themes from "The Grand Canyon Suite"

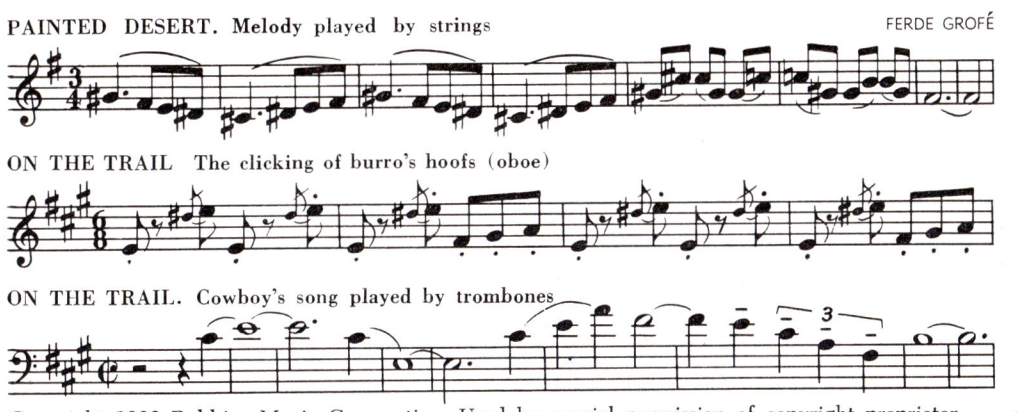

PAINTED DESERT. Melody played by strings

FERDE GROFÉ

ON THE TRAIL The clicking of burro's hoofs (oboe)

ON THE TRAIL. Cowboy's song played by trombones

Copyright 1932 Robbins Music Corporation. Used by special permission of copyright proprietor.

Mountain Trail

WORDS BY RUTH AND THOMAS MARTIN
CZECH FOLK SONG

Snow-capped peaks to climb in the Western ranges, green-turreted hills in the East—both rich in minerals.

Refrain

Melody:
Fol - low me _____ up the trail, _____
Fol - low me, _____ climb - ing high, _____
Come with me _____ far a - bove, _____
Where the moun - tain ea - gles fly. We shall find _____

Harmony:
Fol - low me _____ up the trail,
Fol - low me, climb - ing high,
Come with me far a - bove,
We shall find

10

jour-ney's end _____ When the long trail meets the sky. *Fine*

jour-ney's end When the long trail meets the sky. *Fine*

Verse

1. There far a - bove us, In bright-ness beam - ing,
2. There far be - low us, With joy be - hold - ing.

The snow-capped moun-tain peak is gleam - ing. Through woods and
We see the whole wide world un - fold - ing. The fields and

fields of moun - tain flow - ers, We climb with hearts so
mead - ows flow - er green - ly, Be - neath the blue and

glad and gay; A - cross the wind - swept rock - y
end - less sky. The gold - en sun - shine smiles se -

tow - ers, For - ev - er high - er leads our way.
rene - ly A - bove the moun - tain peaks on high.

D. C. al Fine

11

Fingers of the Sun

TRANSLATED BY DERRICK N. LEHMER
INDIAN SONG FROM THE SOUTHWEST

Drum — *Continue throughout*

The sun is a-rising, A-rising up-on the moun-tains. The sun is a-rising With his hand up-on the moun-tains.

Creation's Morning Song

Here a sun-worshipping song of the Yosemite Indians is contrasted with a morning song by a great composer.

WORDS BY AURELIUS CLEMENS, 5TH CENTURY
MUSIC BY LUDWIG VAN BEETHOVEN

1. Now, with creation's morning song,
Let us, as children of the day,
With wakened heart and purpose strong,
The works of darkness cast away.

2. Oh, may the morn, so pure, so clear,
Its own sweet calm in us instill!
A guileless mind, a heart sincere,
Simplicity of word and will.

The Bell

OLD ENGLISH ROUND

I. The bell doth toll, its echoes roll, I know the sound full well;
II. I love its ringing, for it calls to singing, With its
III. bim, bim, bim, bom, bell, Bim, bim, bim, bom bell.

13

Zuni Sunset Song

WORDS BY CARLOS TROYER
TRADITIONAL SONG OF THE ZUNI INDIANS

This prayer of the Zunis (Pueblo Indians) was chanted to assure night-long protection.

Good night to thee, fair ___ god - dess, We ___ thank thee for thy ___ bless - ing, Good night to thee, fair ___ god - dess, We ___ thank thee for this ___ day. In glo - ry we be - hold thee At ___ ear - ly dawn a - gain. We thank thee for thy ___ bless - ing, To ___ be with us this ___ day. This ___ day, We ___ thank thee ___ for this ___ day. ___

Swift things are beautiful:
Swallows and deer,
And lightning that falls
Bright-veined and clear,
Rivers and meteors,
Wind in the wheat,
The strong-withered horse,
The runner's sure feet.

And slow things are beautiful:
The closing of day,
The pause of the wave
That curves downward to spray,
The ember that crumbles,
The opening flower,
And the ox that moves on
In the quiet of power.
—ELIZABETH COATSWORTH

Many poems have real music in them, waiting to be discovered. You may adventure for a tune by reading a poem aloud, listening to the way the words rise and fall. Autoharp chords sometimes suggest a tune. Note that the poem on this page has a fast part and a slow part.

Moonlight

WORDS BY ALICE WHITE
ITALIAN FOLK SONG (ROUND)

1. While all the world lies dream-ing, I sail the moon-lit wa-ters,
2. The sea and sky are hushed As the waves creep up the sand, Then

A path of sil-ver gleam-ing To guide me on-ward.
a bird, that's hom-ing, brush-es The air a-round me.

Can you see moonlight dancing on water as you listen to this?

Clair de Lune

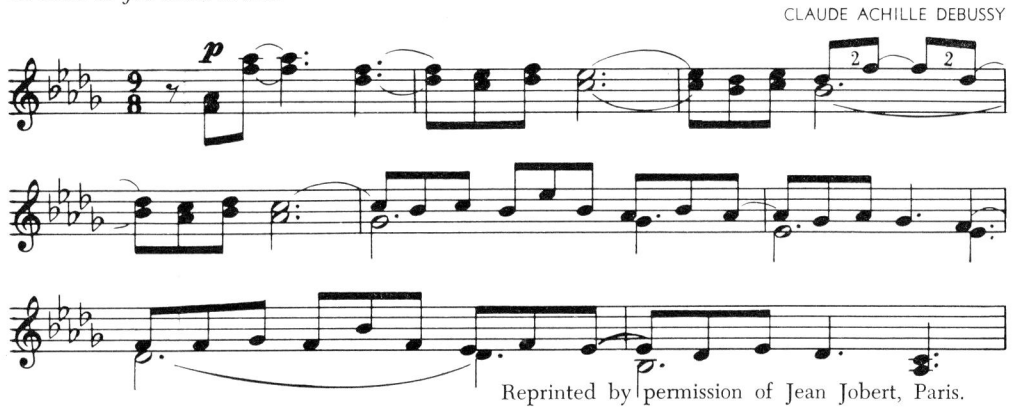

CLAUDE ACHILLE DEBUSSY

Reprinted by permission of Jean Jobert, Paris.

EARLY SETTLERS IN OUR LAND

From Spain

El Alabado

EARLY SOUTHWEST MISSION HYMN

A - la - ba - do y en - sal - za - do
(Ah - lah - bah - doh ee ain - sahl - tha - doh
Lift your heart in joy and ex - alt Him

Se - a el Di - vi - no Sa - cra - men - to,
Say - ah el Dee - bee - noh Sah - crah - main - toh
In the bless - ed Sac - ra - ment ⎯⎯ all Ho - ly,

En quien Di - os o - cul - to a - sis - te
Ain keeain Dee - ohss oh - cool - toh ah - sees - tay.
Where He the Lord, His glo - ry veil - ing,

De las al - mas el ⎯⎯ sus - ten - to.
Day lahs ahl - mahs el ⎯⎯ soos - tain - toh.)
Com - forts souls ⎯⎯ true ⎯⎯ and low - ly.

The priests who came with the early Spanish settlers to the Southwest traveled far from the villages of "New Spain," founding Missions for the Indians. Each Mission church had one or many bells which called the Indians to work or pray. In return for teaching the Spaniards how to raise New World products, the Indians learned how to plant orchards and care for livestock. They were also taught to sing songs of praise. Among these songs was "El Alabado"—a canticle to the sun.

Carillon

FROM THE "L'ARLESIENNE SUITE"
GEORGES BIZET

The Teamster's Song

WORDS BY ELIZABETH BRUCE
SONG FROM SPANISH CALIFORNIA

1. Now dawn comes o'er the moun-tain, Rise up, my ox team, for here's a new day. Night's mist-y shad-ows flee be-fore the day, On with you, my ox-en, plod a-long the way.

2. When night comes down the moun-tain, Rest well, my ox team, your wear-y day done. Your bag of grain you'll have when toil is done, Food and rest for you when fades the set-ting sun.

Refrain
Pull on, my ox team, my pa-tient ox team, Through-out the long day, pull on, my ox team. Plod-ding a-long the road we go, Am-bling, sway-ing, gen-tle ox-en, pull the load. load.

From SPANISH SONGS OF OLD CALIFORNIA by Charles F. Lummis. Copyright assigned to G. Schirmer, Inc. Used by permission. We thank the Southwest Museum of Los Angeles for their help.

My Raincape

WORDS BY MARGARET MARKS
FOLK SONG FROM OLD CALIFORNIA

What's the dif-f'rence If it's rain-ing, Come and take a walk with me. I've a rain-cape, What a rain-cape! Big e-nough for two or three.

In my rain-cape, In my cap-o, In my cap-o, cap-o-tin, We'll be co-sy, Muy con-ten-tos, For the rain-drops can't come in.

Refrain

In my cap-o-tin - tin - tin - tin We'll go walk-ing in the rain,
We can walk all day, and yet,
In my cap-o-tin - tin - tin - tin We'll not hur-ry home a-gain.
There's no dan-ger we'll get wet.

En Roulant Ma Boule

PARAPHRASED BY ADINA WILLIAMSON
FRENCH CANADIAN FOLK SONG

Refrain

En rou-lant ma bou-le rou-lant, En rou-lant ma bou-le.
(Ahn(g) roo-lon(g) mah boo-la roo-lon(g), Ahn(g) roo-lon(g) mah boo-leh.

En rou-lant ma bou-le rou-lant, En rou-lant ma bou-le. *Fine*
Ahn(g) roo-lon(g) mah boo-la roo-lon(g) Ahn(g) roo-lon(g) mah boo-leh.)

Verse

1. Be-hind our house there is a pond, En rou-lant ma bou-le.
2. And ducks play on it all day long, En rou-lant ma bou-le.

Be-hind our house there is a pond, En rou-lant ma bou-le,
And ducks play on it all day long, En rou-lant ma bou-le.

D.C. al Fine

And ducks play on it all day long, Rou-li, rou-lant, ma bou-le rou-lant.
They swim and float and sing this song, Rou-li, rou-lant, ma bou-le rou-lant.

This was the favorite paddling song of the early French settlers who explored the dense forests of the Northeast—using the rivers for roads. Can you hear them making up one verse after another as they skillfully shot rapids and avoided rocks and shoals? They were too busy paddling to make serious verses, so they came back again and again to the refrain line "En roulant ma boule," which means "Roll on, my ball." These early Frenchmen became known as voyageurs (travellers). They were trappers and traders and later acted as guides. Wandering minstrels in fifteenth century France first sang this melody, carrying it about to other countries.

Settlers from France

3. They swim and float and sing this song,
   One day a hunter came along.

4. One day a hunter came along,
   And saw those ducks upon the pond.

5. He saw those ducks upon the pond,
   And scared them so that up they bound.

6. He scared them so that up they bound,
   Their fluffy feathers drifting down.

7. Their fluffy feathers drifting down,
   Down, down, down upon the ground.

8. Down, down, down upon the ground,
   The feathers drifted all around.

9. The feathers drifted all around,
   And made a bed we sleep upon.

Baked Potato

WORDS ADAPTED
FOLK SONG FROM LOUISIANA

Listen to "Cakewalk Ballet Suite," by Hershey Kaye, wherein this and other typically French Louisiana tunes are whipped up for dancing.

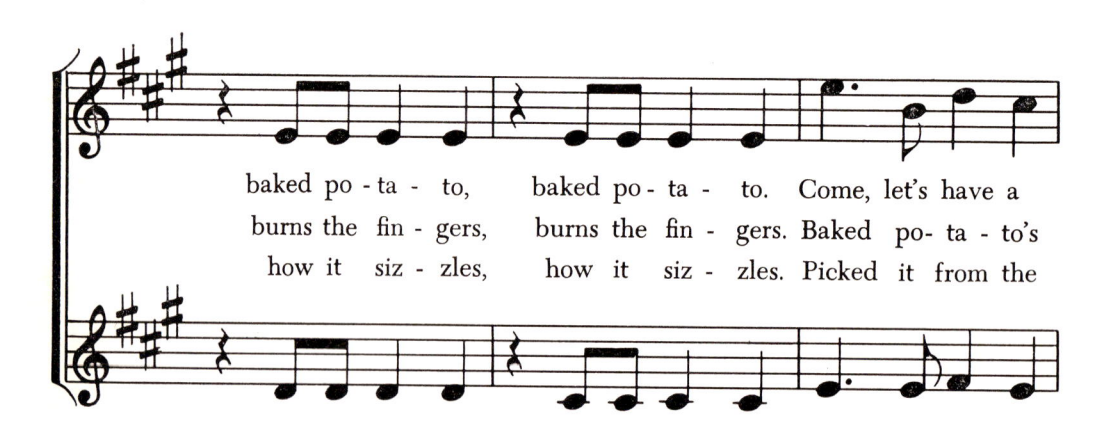

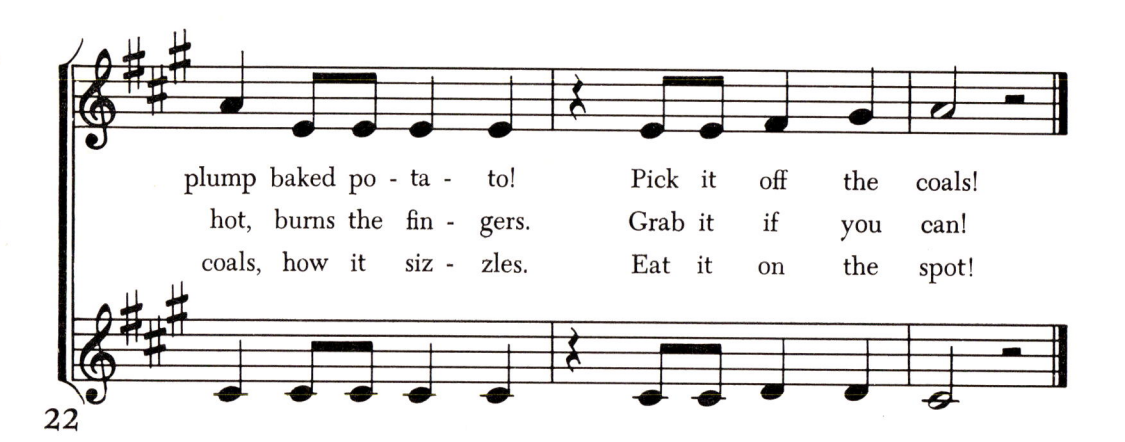

1. Come, let's have a plump baked po-ta-to, baked po-ta-to, baked po-ta-to. Come, let's have a plump baked po-ta-to! Pick it off the coals!
2. Baked po-ta-to's hot, burns the fin-gers, burns the fin-gers, burns the fin-gers. Baked po-ta-to's hot, burns the fin-gers. Grab it if you can!
3. Picked it from the coals, how it siz-zles, how it siz-zles, how it siz-zles. Picked it from the coals, how it siz-zles. Eat it on the spot!

Suzette

French refugees from Canada settled in the bayou country of Louisiana. Some descendents still work in the cane fields or live by shrimp fishing.

WORDS BY LISBETH RAWSKI
FOLK SONG FROM LOUISIANA

O Suzette, dear, { You're keeping me waiting,
                  { Please give me your answer,

O Suzette, { don't you know I'm waiting for you?
           { won't you listen to one so true?

1. I must leave here soon, Suzette, For the sugar fields, my Suzette,
2. I will run the nets, Suzette, On a fishing boat, my Suzette,

I'll cut cane for money to get Pretty things for you.
I'll catch shrimp for money to get Pretty things for you.

Echo

FRENCH ROUND

I. Hear me calling, hear me calling,
II. Echo! Echo!
III. Listen, listen,
IV. Do you hear me calling?

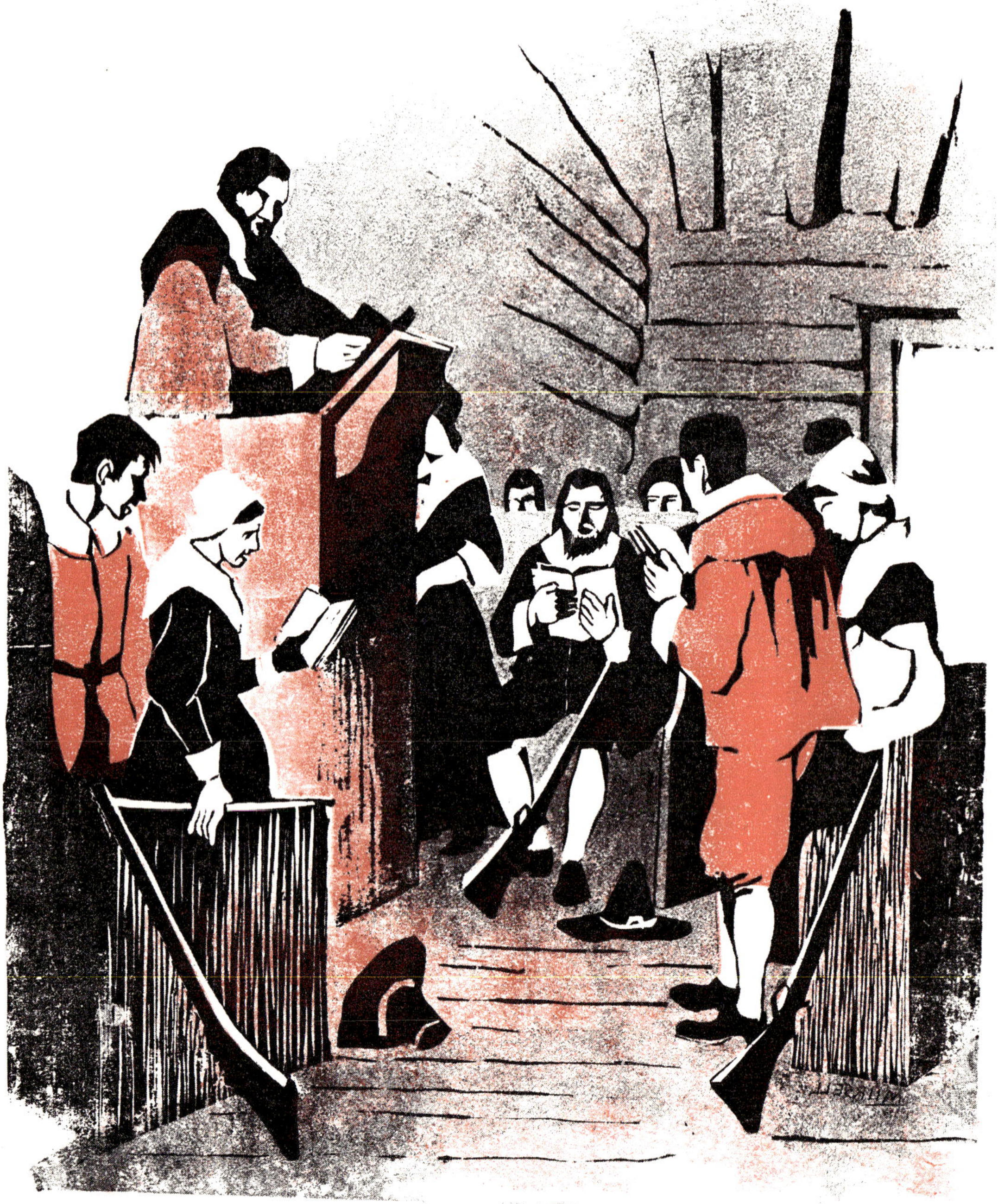

From Old England to New England

Old Hundred

WORDS BY WILLIAM KETHE, 1561
MUSIC BY LOUIS BOURGEOIS, 1551

1. All people that on earth do dwell,
   Sing to the Lord with cheerful voice;
   Him serve with fear, His praise forth tell;
   Come ye before Him and rejoice.

2. The Lord, ye know, is God indeed;
   Without our aid He did us make;
   We are His flock, He doth us feed,
   And for His sheep He doth us take.

3. Oh, enter then His gates with praise,
   Approach with joy His courts unto:
   Praise, laud, and bless His name always,
   For it is seemly so to do.

A band of Pilgrims, setting feet on American shores in 1620 praised God by singing this hymn. They had endured a terrible sea voyage and landed safely in the New World where they could worship God in their own way. The words are a metrical version of the hundredth psalm.

In Good Old Colony Times

FOLK SONG FROM NEW ENGLAND

1. In good old col-o-ny times,
   When we served un-der the king,
   Three ro-guish chaps fell in-to mis-haps,
   Be-cause they could not sing.

2. The first he was a mill-er,
   The second he was a weav-er,
   The third he was a lit-tle tai-lor,
   Three ro-guish chaps to-geth-er.

3. The miller he stole corn,
   The weaver he stole yarn,
   The little tailor he stole broadcloth,
   For to keep these three chaps warm.

4. But the miller got drowned in his pond,
   And the weaver got hanged in his yarn,
   And the little tailor got caught by his claw,*
   With the broadcloth under his arm.

An old legend recast in Yankee tradition—
It takes nine tailors to make a man, but one to make a thief . . .
weavers are unsociable and millers are just no good at all.

*The claw of the Devil.

Jolly Miller

FOLK SONG FROM NEW ENGLAND

1. There was a jol - ly mill - er once lived on the riv - er Dee, He worked and sang from morn till night, No lark more blithe than he.
2. "I love my mill, she is to me Like par - ent, child, and wife. I would not change my sta - tion now with an - y - one in life."

Refrain
And this the bur - den of his song for - ev - er used to be, "I care for no - bod - y, no, not I, If no - bod - y cares for me."

Gay songs as well as religious songs came to New England with the early settlers. Here is a Scottish song, from the river Dee, that tells us how the first millers felt about their millwheels.

27

Chimney Sweeper

STREET CRY ARRANGED BY ROSAMOND JOHNSON

One of these street cries of Colonial tradesmen has been made into a round.

1. Chim - ney sweep-er, sweep out your chim-ney,
Chim - ney sweep-er, know why your chim-ney won't draw?

2. Chimney sweeper, clean out your oven,
   Chimney sweeper, know why your oven won't draw?

3. Chimney sweeper, he sure can make
   Your oven bake, bake, bake a mighty fine cake.

Chairs to Mend

OLD STREET CRY
MUSIC BY WILLIAM HAYES, 1706-1777

I
An - y chairs to mend, old chairs to mend?
Rush or cane bot - toms, old chairs to mend!

II
New mack - er - el, Fresh mack-er-el! New mack - er - el, fresh mack-er-el!

III
An - y old rags, an - y old rags? Here's mon-ey for your old rags!

Past Three O'Clock

WORDS BY JAMES FORTESCUE
ENGLISH FOLK SONG

Past three o'-clock, And a cold frost-y morn-ing,
Past three o'-clock, Good mor-row, mas-ters all.

1. While in your beds you're peace-ful-ly sleep-ing,
2. We go the round, you rest at your lei-sure,
3. When morn-ing breaks, and slum-ber is end-ed,

D.C. al Fine

Un-der the stars our watch we are keep-ing
Safe is your house and safe is your treas-ure.
Give us your thanks, your homes who've de-fend-ed.

Connecticut Peddler

AMERICAN FOLK SONG

*The peddler cries his wares
all in a few long breaths, so no one
else can get a word in edgewise . . .
then his song fades away.*

I'm a ped - dler, I'm a ped - dler, I'm a ped - dler from Con - nect - i - cut, I'm a ped - dler, I'm a ped - dler, And don't you want to buy? Man - y goods have I in store, So lis - ten while I name them o'er. So man - y goods you nev - er saw be - fore, So ver - y man - y goods you nev - er saw be - fore, So lis - ten while I name them o'er.

Here are pins, papers and needles and pins,
Sauce-pans and new baking tins,
Any of which I will sell you. Also,

Here are the seeds of asparagus,
Tid-dle-dum, tid-dle-dee, rum tum, tum,

Lettuce, beets, onions, and peppergrass,
Tid-dle-dum, tid-dle-dee, rum, tum, tum,

Seeds from a well-known society,
Tid-dle-dum, tid-dle-dee, rink-tum-tee,

Seeds of all kinds and variety.
Tid-dle-dum, tid-dle-dee, fad-dle-whee.

Cousin Jedediah

WORDS ANONYMOUS
MUSIC BY H. S. THOMPSON

1. Oh! Ja - cob, get the cows home and put them in the pen,
   For the cous - ins are a - com - ing to see us all a - gain;
   The dow - dy's in the pan, and the tur - key's on the fire,
   And we all must get read - y for Cous - in Jed - e - diah.

2. Now, O - bed, wash your face, boy, and tal - low up your shoes,
   While I go to see Aunt Bet - ty, and tell her all the news;
   And, Kit - ty, slick your hair, and put on your Sun - day gown,
   For Cousin Jed - e - di - ah comes right from Bos - ton town.

Refrain

Cous-in Jed-e-di-ah, There's Hez-e-kiah,
And Az-a-riah, And Aunt So-phia,
And Jed-e-di-ah, All com-ing here to tea;
Oh, won't we have a jol-ly time,
Oh, won't we have a jol-ly time!
Je-ru-sha, put the ket-tle on, We'll all take tea.

Wee Cooper of Fife

FOLK SONG FROM SCOTLAND

Some of these words are nonsense. Others are without their final letters. "Wha" is "what;" "na" is "not;" "woo' " is "wool." "Wee" means "little," "ain," "own." A "cooper" is a man who makes barrels.

1. There was a wee coop-er wha lived i Fife,
   Nick-e-ty, nack-e-ty, noo, noo, noo, And he had got-ten a gen-tle wife,
   Hey, Wil-lie Wal-lack-y, ho, John Dou-gal, a lane quo rush-i-ty roo, ro, ro.

2. She would-na bake, she would-na brew,
   Nick-e-ty, nack-e-ty, noo, noo, noo, For spoil-ing of her come-ly hue,
   Hey, Wil-lie Wal-lack-y, ho, John Dou-gal, a lane quo rush-i-ty roo, ro, ro.

3. She would-na card, she would-na spin,
   Nick-e-ty, nack-e-ty, noo, noo, noo, For the sham-in' o' her gen-tle kin,
   Hey, Wil-lie Wal-lack-y, ho, John Dou-gal, a lane quo rush-i-ty roo, ro, ro.

4. The cooper has gone to his woo' shack,
   And put a sheepskin across his wife's back,

5. I wouldna thrash for your gentle kin,
   But I would thrash my ain sheepskin,

6. Now ye what hae gotten a gentle wife,
   Just send ye for the wee cooper o' Fife.

Soldier, Soldier

In the first verse the soldier protests that he has no coat. For a second verse substitute hat ... then gloves ... then boots, in successive verses. When he says that he is married, the song ends.

FOLK SONG FROM THE APPALACHIAN MOUNTAINS

She: O soldier, soldier, won't you marry me, With your musket, fife, and drum?
He: O no, sweet maid, I cannot marry thee, For I have no coat[1] to put on.

(after fourth verse) have a wife of my own.

Refrain
Then up she went to her grandfather's chest, And got him a coat[1] of the very, very best, She got him a coat[1] of the very, very best, And the soldier put it on.

D.C. al Fine

[2]hat. [3]gloves. [4]boots.

35

Minuet Danced before George Washington

PIERRE LANDRIN DUPORT

The harpsichord still stands in the music room in George Washington's home in Mount Vernon, as shown in the facing picture. This minuet was composed for him and danced there in 1792.

Old England to Old Virginia

The Girl I Left Behind Me

WORDS TRADITIONAL
IRISH MELODY

1. I'm lonesome since I crossed the hill, And o'er the moor and valley. Such heavy thoughts my heart do fill, Since parting with my Sally. I seek no more the fine and gay, For each does but remind me, How swift the hours did pass away, With the girl I left behind me.

2. The bee shall honey taste no more, The dove become a ranger, The dashing waves shall cease to roar Ere she's to me a stranger. But now I'm bound to Brighton camp, Kind heav'n, may favor find me, And send me safely back again To the girl I left behind me.

Irishmen rebelling against British rule infected their enemy with this song. Spreading through England it found its way to America and was sung here during the early wars. Many years later it traveled westward with the pioneers and became a cowboy favorite.

3. My mind her form shall still retain,
   In sleeping or in waking,
   Until I see my love again,
   For whom my heart is breaking.
   If ever I should see the day
   When Mars shall have resigned me,
   For evermore I'll gladly stay
   With the girl I left behind me.

THE COWBOY VERSION

1. I struck the trail in seventy-nine,
   The herd strung out behind me;
   As I jogged along, my mind ran back
   To the gal I left behind me.
   If ever I get off the trail
   And the Indians they don't find me,
   I'll make my way straight back again.
   To the gal I left behind me.

2. When the night was dark and the cattle run,
   With the boys coming on behind me,
   My mind run back at my pistol's crack
   To the gal I left behind me.
   The wind did blow, the rain did flow,
   The hail did fall and blind me;
   I thought of that gal, that sweet little gal,
   That gal I left behind me.

3. She wrote ahead to the place I said,
   I was always glad to find it.
   She says, "I'm true; when you get through,
   Ride back and you will find me."
   That sweet little gal, that true little gal,
   The gal I left behind me!
   That sweet little gal, that true little gal,
   The gal I left behind me!

Wraggle-Taggle Gypsies

OLD ENGLISH BALLAD

*Ballads are story-telling songs.
Many, like this, were brought from
Elizabethan England and cherished here
by successive generations.*

1. There were three gyp-sies a-come to my door, And down-stairs ran
2. Then she pulled off her silk-finished gown, And put on hose
3. It was late last night when my lord came home, In-quir-ing for

this-a la-dy, O! The one sang high, and an-oth-er sang low,
of leath-er, O! The rag-ged rags a-bout our door,
his la-dy, O! The ser-vants said on ev-'ry hand,

And the oth-er sang, "Bon-ny, bon-ny Bis-cay, O!"
And she's gone with the wrag-gle-tag-gle gyp-sies, O!
"She's gone with the wrag-gle-tag-gle gyp-sies, O!"

4. "Come, saddle to me my milk-white steed,
   And go and seek my pony, O!
   That I may ride and seek my bride,
   Who is gone with the wraggle-taggle gypsies, O!"

5. Then he rode high, and he rode low,
   He rode through wood and copses too.
   Until he came to an open field,
   And there he espied his a-lady, O!

6. "What makes you leave your house and land?
   What makes you leave your money, O?
   What makes you leave your new-wedded lord,
   To go with the wraggle-taggle gypsies, O?"

7. "What care I for my house and land?
   And what care I for my money, O?
   What care I for my new-wedded lord?
   I'm off with the wraggle-taggle gypsies, O!"

Golden Slumbers

When the curtains were drawn, shutting out the strange sights and sounds of the New World, lullabies from the Old World put the children to sleep.

WORDS BY THOMAS DECKER
OLD ENGLISH FOLK SONG

1. Gold-en slumbers kiss your eyes,— Smiles a-wait you when you rise;— Sleep, pret-ty loved one, do not cry,— I'll sing lul-la-by, Lul-la-by, I'll sing lul-la-by, lul-la-by.—

2. Cares you know not, go to sleep,— Moth-er here safe watch will keep;— do not cry,— And I will sing a lul-la-by, Lul-la-by, lul-la-by, Lul-la-by!—

Weevily Wheat

AMERICAN FOLK SONG
TUNE FROM AN OLD ENGLISH COUNTRY DANCE

In the Old World, an English country dance. In this country a Virginia Reel and later a western play-party game.

1. Your weevil-y wheat's not fit to eat,
   Neither is your bar-ley; What I want is the best of rye To bake a cake for Char-lie.

2. Charlie's sweet and Charlie's neat;
   Charlie is a dan-dy; Charlie is a nice young man, He feeds the girls on can-dy.

3. Charlie is a brave young man,
   Charlie is a sol-dier; Sword and pistol by his side, His musket on his shoul-der.

Refrain
Rise you up in the morn-ing, All to-geth-er ear-ly;
You need not be at all a-fraid, In-deed I love you dear-ly.

4. Over the river to feed my sheep,
   Over the river to Charlie,
   Over the river to feed my sheep,
   And measure up my barley.

5. The higher up the cherry tree,
   The riper grows the cherry;
   The sooner boys and girls will court,
   The sooner they will marry.

Reuben and Rachel

Girls may take the part of Rachel while boys sing Reuben's lines. Sing it also as a round. Part 2 begins after Part 1 has sung two measures.

WORDS ANONYMOUS
MUSIC TRADITIONAL

1. Reu - ben, Reu - ben, I've been think - ing,
   Oh, my good - ness gra - cious, Ra - chel!
   What a grand world this would be,
   What a queer world this would be,
   If the men were all trans - port - ed
   If the men were all trans - port - ed
   Far be - yond the North - ern Sea.
   Far be - yond the North - ern Sea.

2. Reuben, Reuben, I've been thinking,
   What a gay life girls would lead,
   If they had no men about them,
   None to tease them, none to heed.

   Rachel, Rachel, I've been thinking,
   Men would have a merry time,
   If at once they were transported
   Far beyond the salty brine.

3. Reuben, Reuben, stop your teasing,
   If you've any love for me,
   I was only just a-fooling,
   As I thought of course you'd see.

   Rachel, if you'll not transport us,
   I will take you for my wife,
   And I'll split with you my money
   Every payday of my life.

Settlers from Holland and Germany

The Cutting Bench

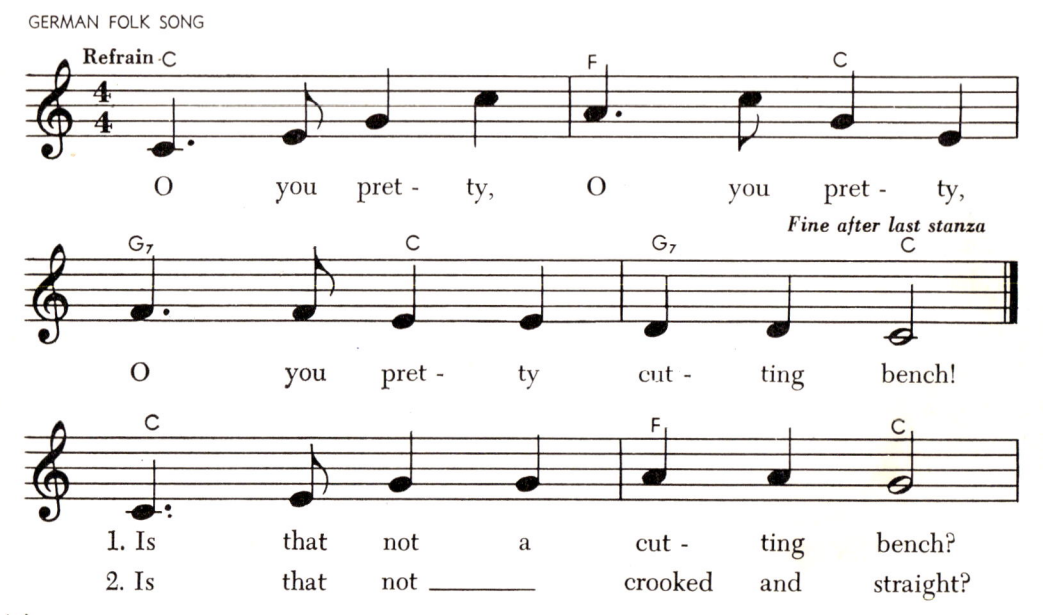

GERMAN FOLK SONG

O you pret - ty, O you pret - ty,
O you pret - ty cut - ting bench!
1. Is that not a cut - ting bench?
2. Is that not crooked and straight?

Yes, that is a cut - ting bench.
Yes, that is ____ crooked and straight.

Is that not ____ short and long?
Is that not a wag - on wheel?

Yes, that is ____ short and long.
Yes, that is a wag - on wheel.

Repeat as many times as necessary

(1.) Short and long, Cut - ting bench.
(2.) { Wag - on wheel, Crooked and straight, }
    { Short and long, Cut - ting bench. }

3. Is that not a long sausage?
   Yes, that is a long sausage.
   Is that not a corn husking?
   Yes, that is a corn husking.

   Corn husking,—Long sausage,
   Wagon wheel,—Crooked and straight,
   Short and long,—Cutting bench.

4. Is that not a large fish?
   Yes, that is a large fish.
   Is that not a small table?
   Yes, that is a small table.

   Small table,—Large fish,
   Corn husking,—Long sausage,
   Wagon wheel,—Crooked and straight,
   Short and long,—Cutting bench.

5. Is that not an ox's tail?
   Yes, that is an ox's tail.
   Is that not a fat goose?
   Yes, that is a fat goose.

   Fat goose,—Ox's tail,
   Small table,—Large fish,
   Corn husking,—Long sausage,
   Wagon wheel,—Crooked and straight,
   Short and long,—Cutting bench.

This song refers to the kind of carpenter's bench used by Pennsylvania Dutch farmers to make furniture and farm implements. Lines 3-6 are sung by two groups as question and answer. All join in spinning out last line to take care of all the words (right, above) to be added, verse by verse.

The Grindstone Man

NEW WORDS AND MUSIC BY JOSEF MARAIS

Sing or play as an introduction

An - y knives, _____ knives to grind. _____

1. Come, friends, and see the whirl - ing wheel by which my
2. A grind - stone man should sharp - en fif - ty knives in

bread I earn; I'll sharp - en well your blade of steel
just an hour; The blaz - ing sun is here a - gain

as my stone wheel I turn. I have to keep my
to rob me of my power. I need a lit - tle

wife and child in shel - ter when the wind is wild.
rest, you know, That's why the mon - ey comes in slow.

Ti - li - di - pum - ti - la, The blade up - on the
Ti - li - di - pum - ti - la, I need a shirt, you

grind - stone I put while I ped - al with my foot.
need a _____ dress, so I ped - al with my foot.

46

Refrain

Yup yup yup yup yup yup yup yup yup yup yup yup yup,
An-y knives, _____ knives to grind, _____
Knives to grind, _____ knives to grind. _____

Copyright 1956, Fideree Music Corporation, New York, N. Y. Used by permission.

Sweep the Floor

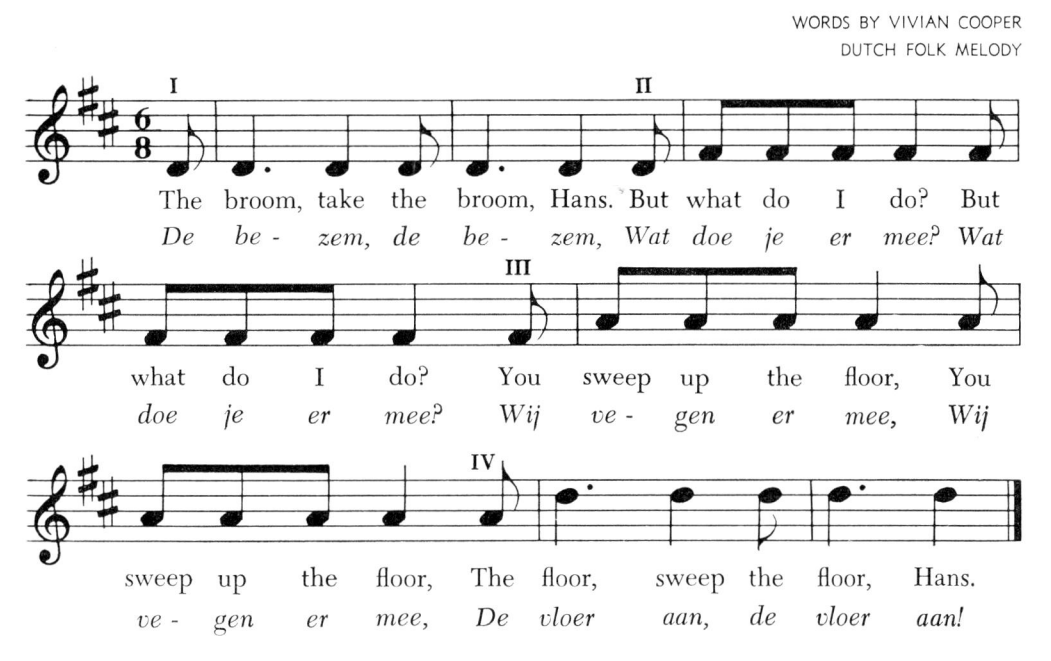

WORDS BY VIVIAN COOPER
DUTCH FOLK MELODY

I. The broom, take the broom, Hans. II. But what do I do? But what do I do? III. You sweep up the floor, You sweep up the floor, IV. The floor, sweep the floor, Hans.

De be-zem, de be-zem, Wat doe je er mee? Wat doe je er mee? Wij ve-gen er mee, Wij ve-gen er mee, De vloer aan, de vloer aan!

This four-part round from Holland has a very amusing sound sung in Dutch. This is how the words are pronounced: Bezem, bayzum; je, ya; mee, may; vegen, faygan; doe, doo; er, air; wij, way; vloer, fluur. When we know that bezem is the Dutch word for "broom" we can easily guess what the other words mean.

O Morning Star

WORDS BY NANCY BYRD TURNER
MUSIC BY JOHANN SEBASTIAN BACH

1. O Morn-ing Star, thou Love of God, Thy beau-ty bright-ens all our road, It shines on hill and hol-low. The world was dark in oth-er days, But now, O Morn-ing Star, thy rays Are clear for us to fol-low. Ho-ly! Ho-ly! Night has end-ed, fair and splen-did Light is show-ing, We are safe in all our go-ing.

2. O Star, a-bove an hum-ble town A-cross the world, thy light came down Long years a-go, and pure-ly That light shines on up-on our way, It guides our trust-ing feet to-day, And still will lead us sure-ly. Ho-ly! Ho-ly! Star of morn-ing, sky a-dorn-ing, Fail-ing nev-er, Love of God, to lead us ev-er.

Before Bach's day, only the choir sang in the churches. In order to encourage the people to join in the singing, Bach took some of the fine tunes that they knew and arranged them for church use. These are known as "Bach chorales." The 🐛's, above, tell us to prolong these notes.

WORKERS BUILD AMERICA – *Gathering Nature's Bounty*

I hear America singing, the varied carols I hear;
Those of mechanics—each one singing his, as it should be,
        blithe and strong;
The carpenter singing his, as he measures his plank or beam,
The mason singing his, as he makes ready for work, or leaves off work;
The boatman singing what belongs to him in his boat—the deck-hand singing
        on the steamboat deck;
The shoemaker singing as he sits on his bench—the hatter singing as he stands;
The wood-cutter's song—the ploughboy's, on his way in the morning,
        or at the noon intermission, or at sundown;
The delicious singing of the mother—or of the young wife at work—
        or of the girl sewing or washing;
Each singing what belongs to him or her, and to none else; . . . .
                    —WALT WHITMAN

In the Sugar Camp

TRANSLATED BY FREDERICK BURTON
OJIBWAY INDIAN SONG

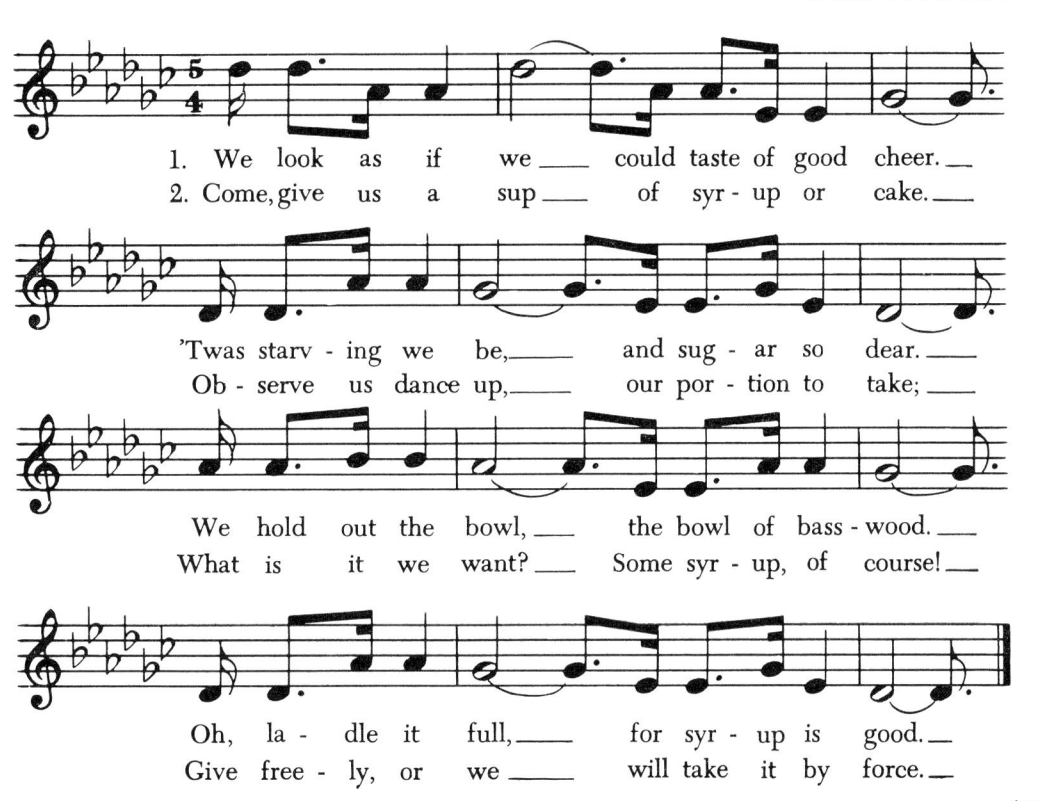

1. We look as if we could taste of good cheer.
   'Twas starv-ing we be, and sug-ar so dear.
   We hold out the bowl, the bowl of bass-wood.
   Oh, la-dle it full, for syr-up is good.

2. Come, give us a sup of syr-up or cake.
   Ob-serve us dance up, our por-tion to take;
   What is it we want? Some syr-up, of course!
   Give free-ly, or we will take it by force.

Lumberman's Alphabet

AMERICAN FOLK SONG

This song had only six verses for a long time. Then some inventive lumberjack added a seventh.

1. A is for Ax, and that we all know,
And B is for Boy that can use it al - so;
C is for Chop - ping we first do be - gin,
And D is for Dan - ger we of - ten fall in.

Refrain
So mer - ry, _____ so mer - ry are we,
No mor - tals on earth are as hap - py as we.
To me I der - ry O der - ry I der - ry down,
Use shan - ty boys well and there's noth - ing goes wrong.

2. E is for Echo that through the woods rang,
   And F is for Foreman, the head of our gang;
   G is for Grindstone at night we do turn,
   And H is for Handle so smoothly worn.

3. I is for Iron which we mark our pine,
   And J is for Jovial we're always incline';
   K is for Keen Edge our axes we keep,
   And L is for Lice that keep us from sleep.

4. M is for Moss which we chink our camp,
   And N is for Needle with which we mend our pants;
   O is for Owl which hooted at night,
   And P is for Pine which we always fall right.

5. Q is for Quickness we put ourselves to,
   R is for River we haul the logs to;
   S is for Sleds we haul the logs on,
   T is for Team that pulls them along.

6. U is for Uses we put ourselves to,
   And V is for Valley we haul the logs through;
   And W is for Woods we leave in the spring,
   And now I have sung all I'm going to sing.

7. X is for Christmas when the yarding's all done,
   Y is for Yonder, the set of the sun;
   Zed is for Zero, in the cold winter time,
   And now I have brought all these letters in rhyme.

Lumberman's Song

FINNISH FOLK SONG

A nonsense song proving that men like to joke about things near and dear to them.

1. My sweetheart is a gorgeous gal, Though she's thin and bony;
   My sweetheart is a gorgeous gal, Though she's thin and bony.
   Hey loo-lee-a, il-lal-la, Though she's thin and bony;
   Hey loo-lee-a, il-lal-la, Though she's thin and bony.

2. My gal's head is small and neat, Though it's slightly crooked;
   My gal's head is small and neat, Though it's slightly crooked.
   Hey loo-lee-a, il-lal-la, Though it's slightly crooked;
   Hey loo-lee-a, il-lal-la, Though it's slightly crooked.

3. My gal's hair is dark, dark brown,
   But she never combs it.
   My gal's hair is dark, dark brown,
   But she never combs it.
   Hey loo-lee-a, il-lal-la,
   But she never combs it.

4. My sweetheart has bright blue eyes,
   But they cross each other.
   My sweetheart has bright blue eyes,
   But they cross each other.
   Hey loo-lee-a, il-lal-la,
   But they cross each other.

5. When we go to the market-place,
   Even horses laugh at her.
   When we go to the market-place,
   Even horses laugh at her.
   Hey loo-lee-a, ha! ha! ha!
   Even horses laugh at her.

Bigerlow

Men sang lustily on the barges carrying raw products east and manufactured goods back west.

SONG OF THE GREAT LAKES BOATMEN

'Twas one Oc-to-ber morn-in' That I saw a won-drous sight;

'Twas the tim-ber dro-ver "Big-er-low," A-hail-in' from De-troit.

Watch her! Catch her! Jump up in her Ju-ju-ba-ju!

Give her the sheet an' let her go, We're the boys to see her through!

You should a' heard her howl-in' When the wind was blow-in' free!

'Twas on the trip to Buf-fa-lo from Mil-wau-kee!

Before the days of lake steamers (1890) barges called "timber drovers" carried timber and other raw products from the shores of Lake Michigan to Buffalo—an industrial area. These barges were under sail. "Give her the sheet" meant to unfurl more sail in order to increase speed.

Cumberland Mountain Bear Chase

CUMBERLAND MOUNTAIN FOLK SONG

Refrain

A-way, a-way, we're bound for the moun-tain, bound for the moun-tain, bound for the moun-tain! O-ver the hill, the fields and the foun-tain, a-way, to the chase, a-way, a-way.

Verse

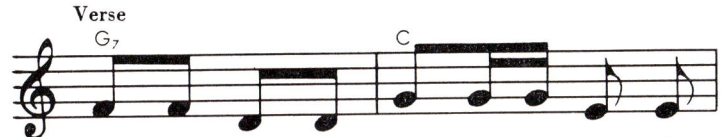

1. Now we're set just right for the race, the old hound dogs are ready for the chase,
2. Rov-er, Rov-er, see him, see him, Rov-er, Rov-er, catch him, catch him,
3. Listen to the hound dog's heav-y bay, Sound-ing high o-ver the way,
4. All night long till break of dawn, Mer-ri-ly the chase goes on,

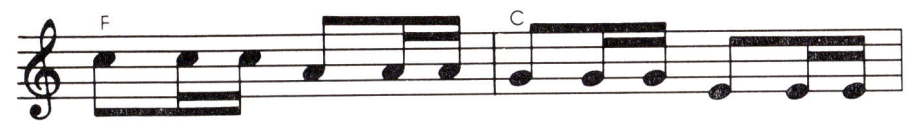

O-ver the moun-tain, the fields and the foun-tain, a-way to the chase a-way, a-way.

Fishing Boats

WORDS BY RUTH MARTIN
PORTUGUESE FOLK SONG

Portuguese were among the first fishermen to discover the wonderful fishing grounds off the northeastern coast of America.

1. In the ear-ly spring-time when the win-ter storms have end-ed, All our vil-lage fish-er-men pre-pare to go to sea. Ev-'ry boat is paint-ed bright-ly, all the nets are new-ly mend-ed. All the fleet is rid-ing light-ly in the friend-ly har-bor's lea. Oh, Now the fish-er-men are read-y, friends are there to speed their go-ing, And a stead-y

2. As the crowd is wait-ing comes the sound of church bells peal-ing, Then the vil-lage priest ap-pears to bless the fleet to-day. He is stand-ing there be-side them, where the fish-er-men are kneel-ing, "'May the Light of Heav-en guide them,' we at home will al-ways pray." Oh, Now the fish-ing fleet is sail-ing, may the bright-est stars pro-tect them, May un-fail-ing

56

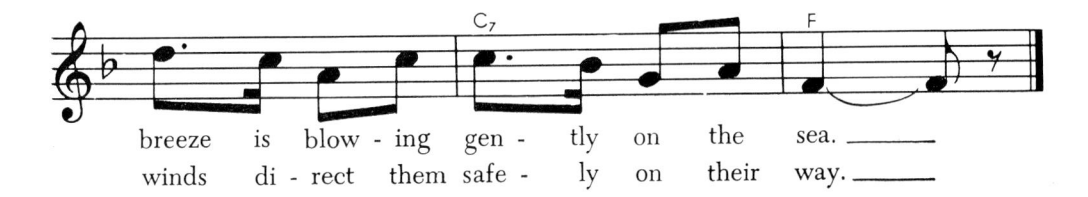

breeze is blow - ing gen - tly on the sea.
winds di - rect them safe - ly on their way.

Ground Hog

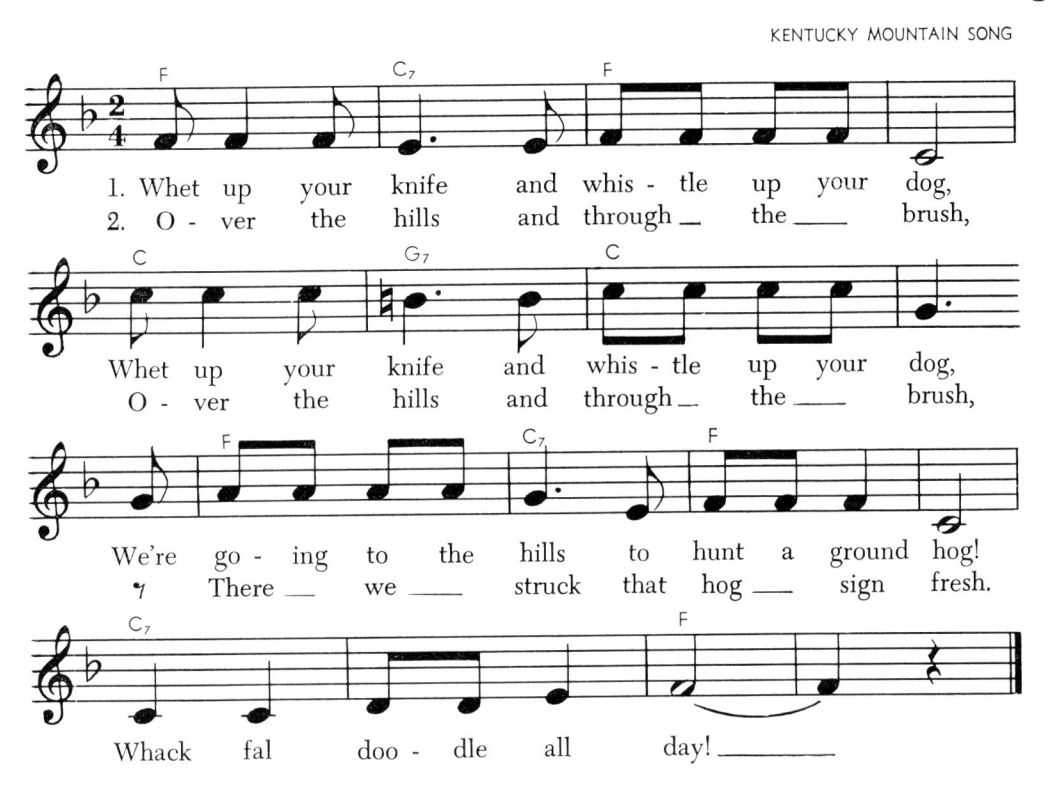

KENTUCKY MOUNTAIN SONG

1. Whet up your knife and whis - tle up your dog,
2. O - ver the hills and through the brush,

Whet up your knife and whis - tle up your dog,
O - ver the hills and through the brush,

We're go - ing to the hills to hunt a ground hog!
There we struck that hog sign fresh.

Whack fal doo - dle all day!

3. Up came Berry with a ten foot pole,
   And roused it in that ground hog hole.

4. Took him by the tail and wagged him to a log,
   And swore, by grab, it's a pretty fine hog.

5. Work, boys, work as hard as you can tear,
   The meat'll do to eat and the hide'll do to wear.

6. Work, boys, work for all you'll earn,
   Skin after night and tan him in a churn.

7. They put him in a pot and the children began to smile,
   They ate that ground hog before it struck a boil.

8. Up stepped Susie with a snicker and a grin,
   Ground hog grease all over her chin.

The Whale

OLD SEA CHANTEY

1. 'Twas in eighteen hundred and fifty three
And of June the thirteenth day,
That our gallant ship her anchor weighed,
And for Greenland bore away, brave boys,
And for Greenland bore away.

2. The lookout in the crosstrees stood,
   With his spyglass in his hand.
   "There's a whale, there's a whale, there's a whalefish," he cried,
   "And she blows at every span, brave boys,
   And she blows at every span."

3. The captain stood on the quarter-deck,
   And a fine little man was he.
   "Overhaul! Overhaul! Let your davit-tackles fall,
   And launch your boats for sea, brave boys,
   And launch your boats for sea."

4. Now the boats were launched and the men aboard,
   And the whale was in full view;
   Resolv-ed was each seaman bold
   To steer where the whalefish blew, brave boys,
   To steer where the whalefish blew.

5. We struck that whale, the line paid out,
   But she gave a flourish with her tail;
   The boat capsized and four men were drowned,
   And we never caught that whale, brave boys,
   And we never caught that whale.

Abalone

FOLK SONG FROM CALIFORNIA

The abalone is a large single shellfish found on the West Coast. "Lazzaroni" is the plural form of an Italian word for "beggar."

Verse
1. In Monterey the people say, "We feed the lazzaroni; On caramels and cockle shells and hunks of abalone."

Refrain
Abalone, Abalone,
Melody
Abalone, Abalone, Abalone, And hunks of abalone.
lone, And hunks of abalone.

2. O, some folks boast of quail on toast,
   Because they think it's toney;
   But my big cat gets nice and fat
   On hunks of abalone.

3. I telegraph my better half
   By Morse or by Marconi;
   But when in need of greater speed
   I send an abalone.

4. Our naval hero, best of all,
   His name was Pauley Joney;
   He sailed the sea just as he pleased,
   But he never ate abalone.

Old Joe Clark

AMERICAN FIDDLIN' TUNE

1. I went up on a mountain top To give my horn a blow; Thought I heard the preacher say, "Yonder comes old Joe."
2. Old Joe Clark he had a house Was sixteen stories high; Ev'ry story in that house Was filled with chicken pie.
3. I went down to Old Joe's house, Never been there before; He slept on a feather-bed, I slept on the floor.

Refrain

Fare you well, old Joe Clark, Fare you well, I'm gone.

Fare you well, old Joe Clark, better be getting on.

Down in a Coal Mine

PENNSYLVANIA COAL MINERS' SONG

*There's an Irish lilt to this.
Many Irish settlers helped
to bring up coal from the mines.*

1. I am a jovial collier lad, and blithe as blithe can be,
For let the times be good or bad they're all the same to me;
'Tis little of the world I know and care less for its ways,
For where the Dog Star never glows, I wear away my days.

Refrain
Down, down in a coal mine, underneath the ground,
Where a gleam of sunshine never can be found;
Digging dusky diamonds all the season round,
Down, down in a coal mine, underneath the ground.

62

2. My hands are horny, hard and black with working in the vein,
   And like the clothes upon my back my speech is rough and plain;
   Well, if I stumble with my tongue I've one excuse to say,
   'Tis not the collier's heart that's wrong, 'tis the head that goes astray.

3. So cheer up, lads, and make ye much of every joy ye can;
   Now let your mirth be always such as best becomes a man;
   However fortune turns about we'll still be jovial souls,
   For what would America be without the lads that look for coals.

My Sweetheart's the Mule in the Mines

PENNSYLVANIA COAL MINERS' SONG

My sweet-heart's the mule in the mines,
I drive her with-out an-y lines.
On the bump-er I stand, With my whip in my hand.
My sweet-heart's the mule in the mines.

Before electricity was installed underground, mules were used to pull the flat-cars that transport mined coal from the digging area to the shaft up which it is lifted to the surface. Boys in their early teens drove these mules. Early in the morning they got their mules from the stables, fed them, then hitched them to "trips" of empty cars. With a crack of the whip and a shout, each mule train started off down a passage so dark only the mule could see what lay ahead. Thus, the driver had no reins; he had to govern his mule with the tone of his voice. The boys had to work underground for ten hours. They sang this and other songs to brighten the long day.

Harvests and Herds

O the farmer's joys!
. . . . . .
. . . . . .
To plough land in the fall for winter-sown crops,
To plough land in the spring for maize,
To train orchards—to graft the trees—to gather apples in the fall.
—WALT WHITMAN

The Cotton Song

GROUP OF CHILDREN, UNIVERSITY SCHOOL
MINNEAPOLIS, MINNESOTA

1. Pick cotton, pick cotton, All the way,
   all the day, Pick cotton, pick cotton,
   On the way to heaven.

2. Keep going, keep going, On the way,
   all the way, Keep going, keep going,
   On the way to heaven.

3. Come join us, come join us,
   On this day, all the way,
   Come join us, come join us,
   On the way to Heaven.

Choppin'

WORK SONG COLLECTED BY J. ROSAMOND JOHNSON

Huh! He's a-chop-pin' in the new ground,

Huh! He's a-chop-pin' in the new ground,

Huh! He's a-chop-pin' in the new ground,

Glo-ry hal-le-lu-jah! Ear-ly in the morn-ing

He's a-chop-pin' in the new ground,

Chop-pin' till the sun's gone down. Oh, hal-le-lu-jah!

Boll Weevil

FOLK SONG FROM SOUTHERN UNITED STATES

1. The boll wee-vil is a lit-tle black bug, Come from Mex-i-co, they say, Come all the way to Tex-as, Just a-look-ing for a place to stay.
2. The first time I saw the boll weevil, He was sit-ting on the square. The next time I saw the boll weevil, He had all his fam-'ly there.

Refrain
Just a-look-ing for a home, Just a-look-ing for a home. Just a-look-ing for a home, Just a-look-ing for a home.

The flower on the cotton plant turns red, falls away, and cotton grows in the pod. Here in this "boll," the boll weevil finds a snug home with food at hand. Spreading up from Mexico, weevils ruined many a cotton crop. Today, planes spray the fields.

3. The farmer took the boll weevil
   And he put him in hot sand.
   The boll weevil said, "This is mighty hot,
   But, I'll stand it like a man,
   This'll be my home,"

4. The farmer took the boll weevil,
   And he put him on a lump of ice.
   The weevil said to the farmer,
   "This is mighty cool and nice,
   This'll be my home,"

5. The merchant got half the cotton,
   The boll weevil got the rest;
   Didn't leave the farmer's wife,
   But one old cotton dress,
   And it's full of holes,

6. The farmer said to his missus,
   "Now what you think of that?
   The boll weevil has made a nest
   In my best Sunday hat,
   He's got a home,"

Peanut Picking Song

FOLK SONG FROM SUFFOLK COUNTY, VIRGINIA

Peanuts (goober peas) develop underground. The entire vine is dug up and "shocked." When dry, the peanuts are picked off.

Refrain

You can do just-a what you please, —
I'm goin' to pick me some goo-ber peas, —
I'm goin' to pick me some goo-ber peas, — And then I'm goin' home.

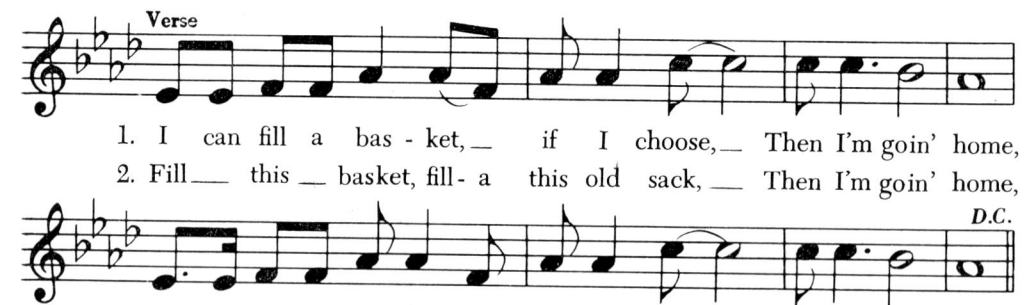

Verse

1. I can fill a bas-ket, — if I choose, — Then I'm goin' home,
2. Fill — this — basket, fill-a this old sack, — Then I'm goin' home,

Boss is going to give me-a Christ-mas shoes, — Then I'm goin' home.
The old — boss-man fetch me when he gets back, — Then I'm goin' home.

3. Two red han'k'chiefs and a walkin' cane,
   Then I'm goin' home,
   Then I'm goin' to strut down the Big House lane,
   Then I'm goin' home.

4. Send me to the Big House for to get off that rack,
   Then I'm goin' home,
   His old coat for to put on my back,
   Then I'm goin' home.

From THE NEW AMERICAN SONG BOOK by Marx and Anne Oberndorfer, copyright 1933-1941 by Hall & McCreary Company. Used by permission.

5. See that big old possum there up in the tree,
   Then I'm goin' home,
   Bet that he's awaitin' up there for me,
   Then I'm goin' home.

6. I'm goin' to catch him unless he flies,
   Then I'm goin' home,
   Then we'll talk about some old dumplin' pies,
   Then I'm goin' home.

Shepherds Go with Their Flocks

WORDS BY MARGARET MARKS
FRENCH FOLK SONG

1. Oh-ay, oh-ay, oh-ay! At the break of the day,
   Oh-ay, oh-ay, oh-ay! At the crow of the cock,
   Up the steep mountain highway
   Shepherds go with their flocks. Sometimes the lambs stray in byways, And they play on the rocks.

2. Oh-ay, oh-ay, oh-ay! When the twilight is gray,
   Oh-ay, oh-ay, oh-ay! Feared of wolf and of fox,
   Shepherds go down the highway
   With their fleecy white flocks. Sometimes the lambs stray in byways, And they play on the rocks.

69

Ah, Lovely Meadows

TRANSLATED FROM THE CZECH
CZECH FOLK SONG

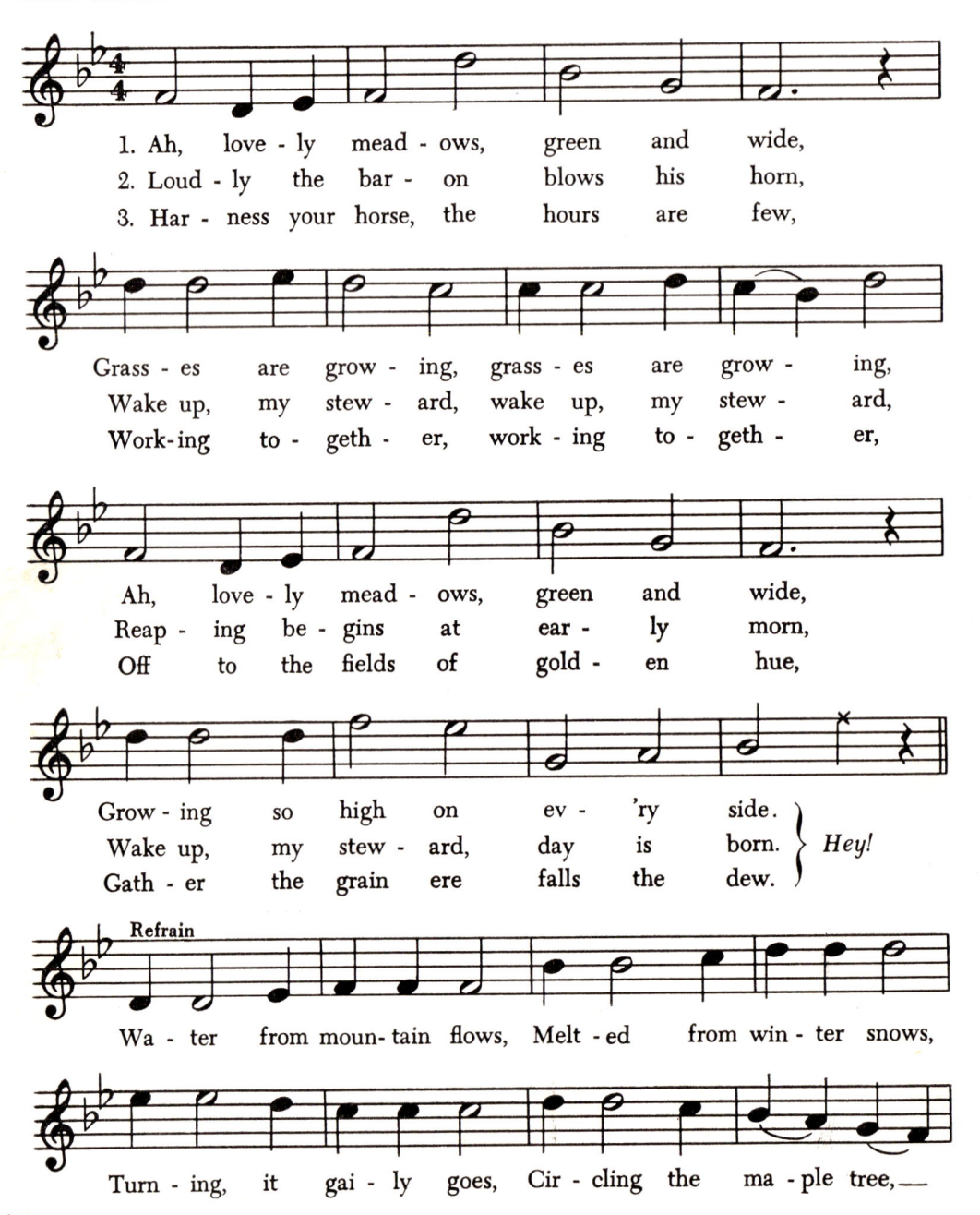

*Wheat now waves and corn grows tall
in the heartland of America—
once a vast meadow dotted with buffalo.*

1. Ah, lovely meadows, green and wide,
   Grasses are growing, grasses are growing,
   Ah, lovely meadows, green and wide,
   Growing so high on ev'ry side.
2. Loudly the baron blows his horn,
   Wake up, my steward, wake up, my steward,
   Reaping begins at early morn,
   Wake up, my steward, day is born. } *Hey!*
3. Harness your horse, the hours are few,
   Working together, working together,
   Off to the fields of golden hue,
   Gather the grain ere falls the dew.

Refrain

Water from mountain flows, Melted from winter snows,
Turning, it gaily goes, Circling the maple tree,—

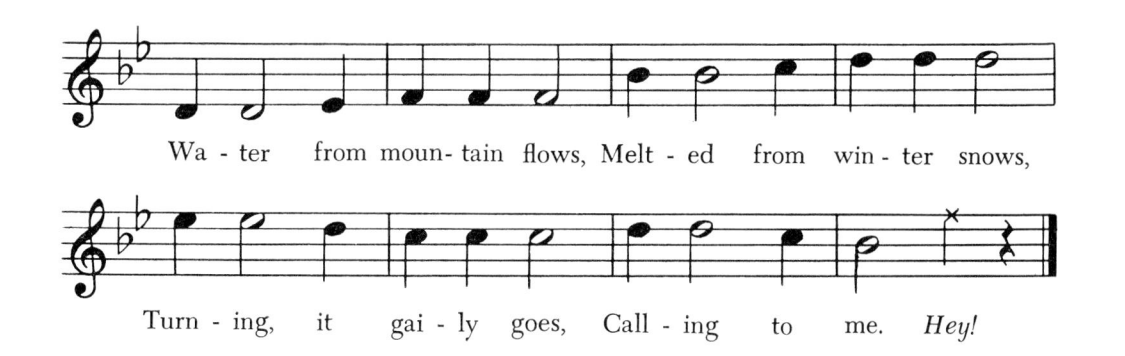

Wa - ter from moun - tain flows, Melt - ed from win - ter snows, Turn - ing, it gai - ly goes, Call - ing to me. *Hey!*

Wheat Fields

WORDS BY JAMES S TIPPETT
MUSIC BY MILTON KAYE

Yel - low wheat, yel - low wheat, When the wind blows You are a sea of gold - en waves, Where a pi - rate goes. The reap - er is the pi - rate who takes your gold - en store, And leaves a field of stub - ble where you were waves be - fore.

71

The Lemon Tree

TRANSLATED BY ROBERTA McLAUGHLIN AND BESSIE STANCHFIELD
LATIN-AMERICAN FOLK SONG

She perched in the green lem-on tree, the bird
Y es-ta-ba la pá-jar-a pin - ta
(Ee es-tah- bah lah pah-hahr-ah peen - tah

with col-ors so love-ly to see,
sen - ta - da en su ver - de li - mon,
sen - tah - dah ain soo vair - day lee - mohn,

With her bright yel-low bill, she pecked and pecked
Con el pi - co re - co - ge las flor - es,
Cohn el pee - coh ray - coh - gay lahs floor - aiss,

the leaves of the green lem-on tree.
Con el pi - co re - co - ge el a - mor.
Cohn el pee - coh ray - coh - gay el ah - mohr.

Ay, ay, ay, ay! The flow-ers are fair to
Ay, ay, ay, ay! En don - de la en-cuen - tro
I, I, I, I! Ain dohn - day lah ain-kwain-troh

72

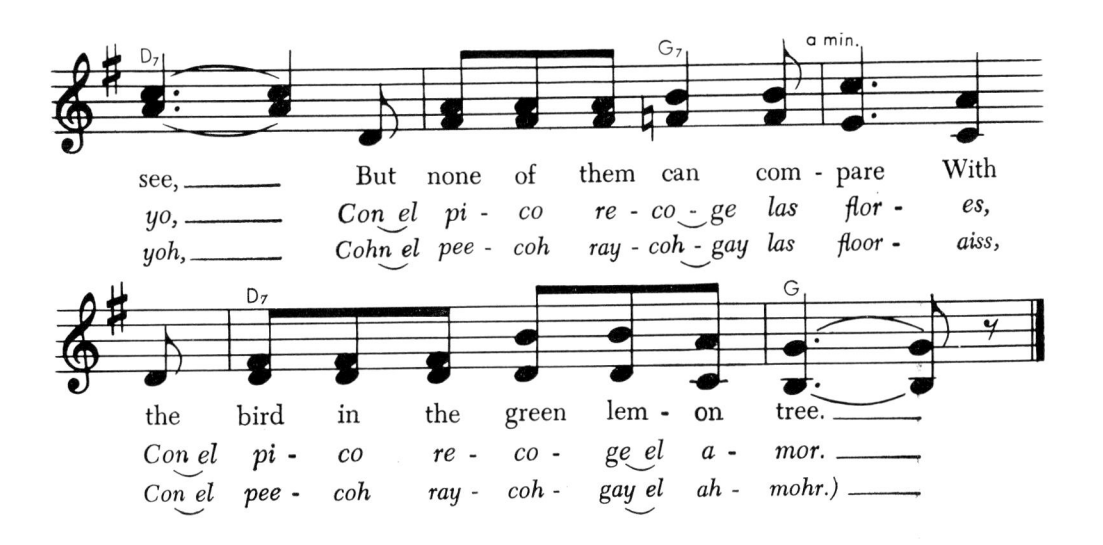

see, ____ But none of them can com-pare With
yo, ____ Con el pi-co re-co-ge las flor-es,
yoh, ____ Cohn el pee-coh ray-coh-gay las floor-aiss,

the bird in the green lem-on tree. ____
Con el pi-co re-co-ge el a-mor. ____
Con el pee-coh ray-coh-gay el ah-mohr.) ____

Early explorers in the Americas found the Indians growing corn. Corn is now our most valuable crop.

My Corn Seeds

TRANSLATED BY RALPH HESS
PAPAGO INDIAN SONG

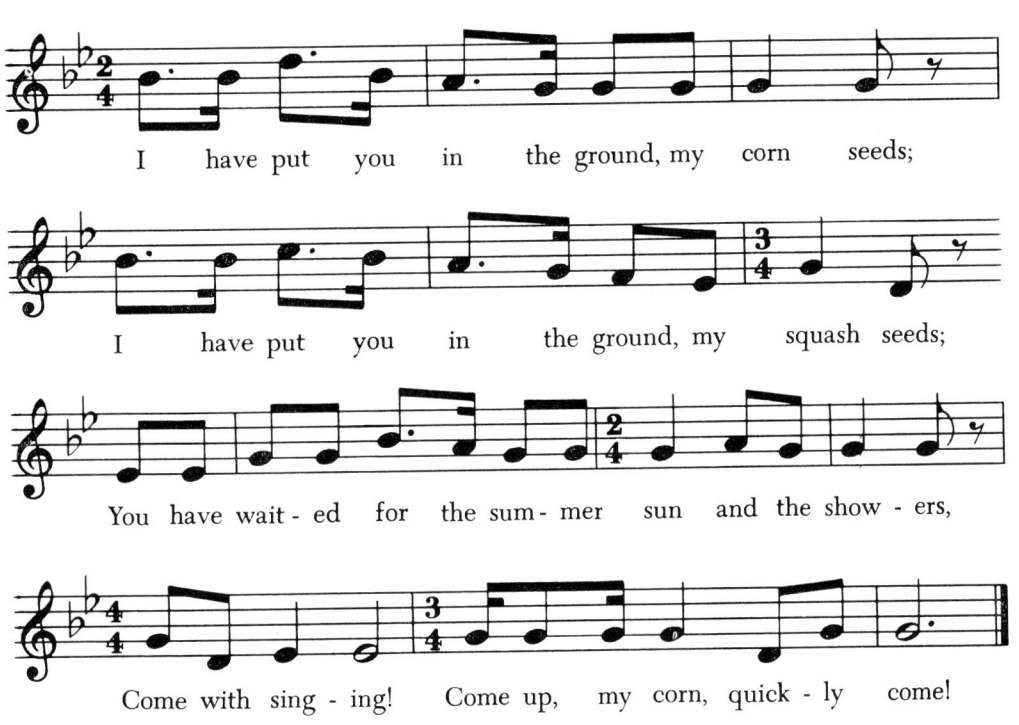

I have put you in the ground, my corn seeds;

I have put you in the ground, my squash seeds;

You have wait-ed for the sum-mer sun and the show-ers,

Come with sing-ing! Come up, my corn, quick-ly come!

73

Music in the Barn

PLAY-PARTY SONG

Mis-sy in the barn, The barn, oh, lear-y, Sweet-est lit-tle Mis-sy I ev-er did see, Oh, *bonne, bonne,* Won't you be my part-ner, Say, lit-tle Mis-sy, Won't you dance with me? Step back, gal, Don't you come near-er, All those sas-sy words you say, Oh, *bonne, bonne,* Won't you be my part-ner, Say, lit-tle Mis-sy, Won't you dance with me?

In the early autumn, when the corn was safe in the barn, the farmer could relax and play a little. Even then business was mixed with pleasure, as whole communities met first on one farm and then another for corn-husking bees. The man who shucked an ear with red kernels could kiss any girl at the party. The French word "bonne" (pronounced bonn), is a short version of "my good lady."

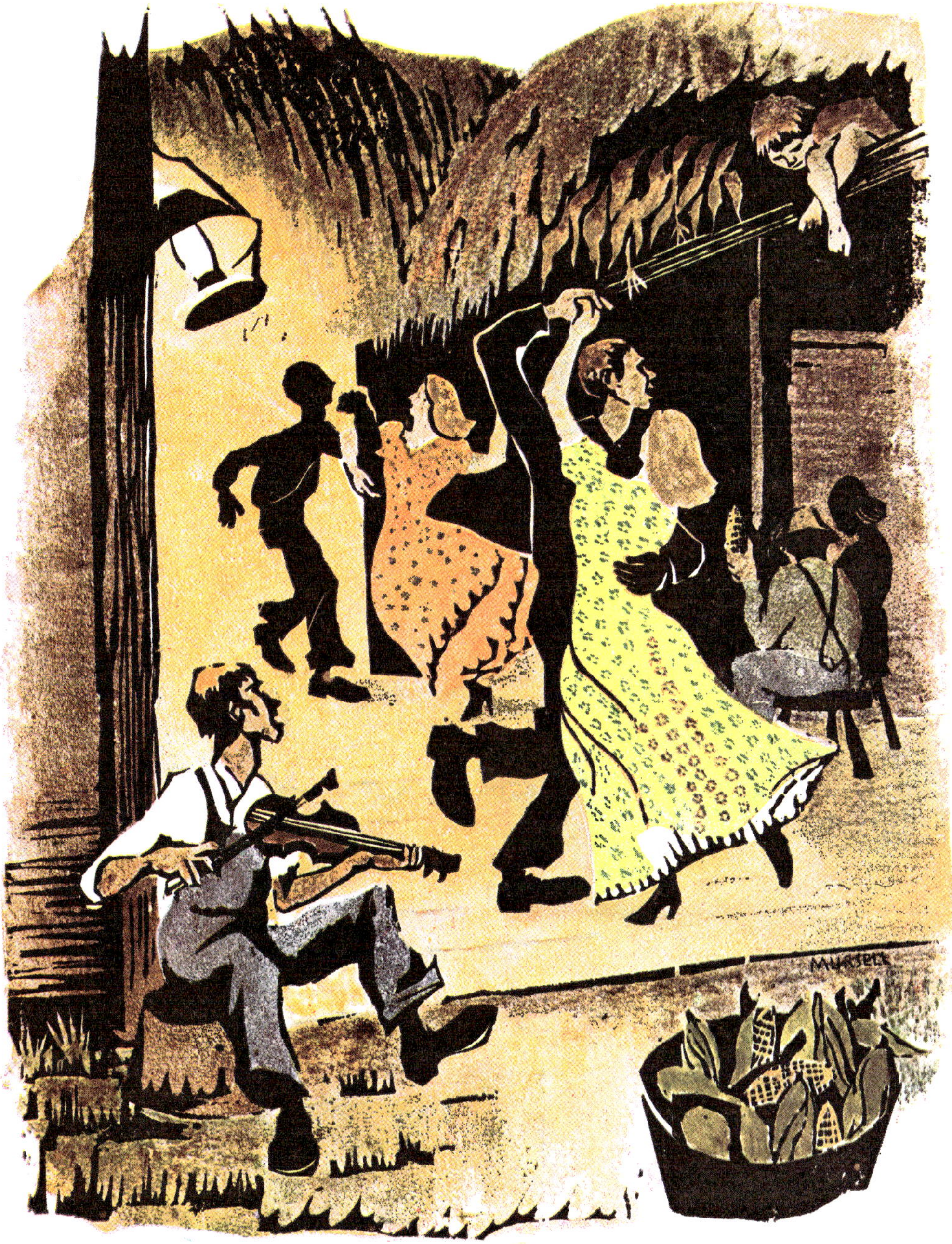
MURSELL

Tic-Tì, Tic-Tà

ADAPTED FROM THE ITALIAN
MUSIC BY GAETANO LAMA

*Many Italians brought to this land
a wonderful gift for planting orchards
and getting vineyards to produce abundantly.*

Sun - shine is smil - ing o - ver hill, o - ver dale,
Doves on the wing are float - ing down from on high,

O - ver vine - yards and or - chards to - day;
Gen - tly coo - ing, they light here and there,

Boun - te - ous har - vest, ev - 'ry bas - ket and pail,
Bring - ing the az - ure from the hue of the sky,

Brim - ming full for the fes - ti - val ar - ray
Mak - ing

har - vest and fes - ti - val more fair. Turn and re - turn, like the
Sing like a king, let the

flow'r and the fern, To my heart, tic - a - tì, tic - a - tà,
gay dan - cers swing To the tune, tic - a - tì, tic - a - tà,

76

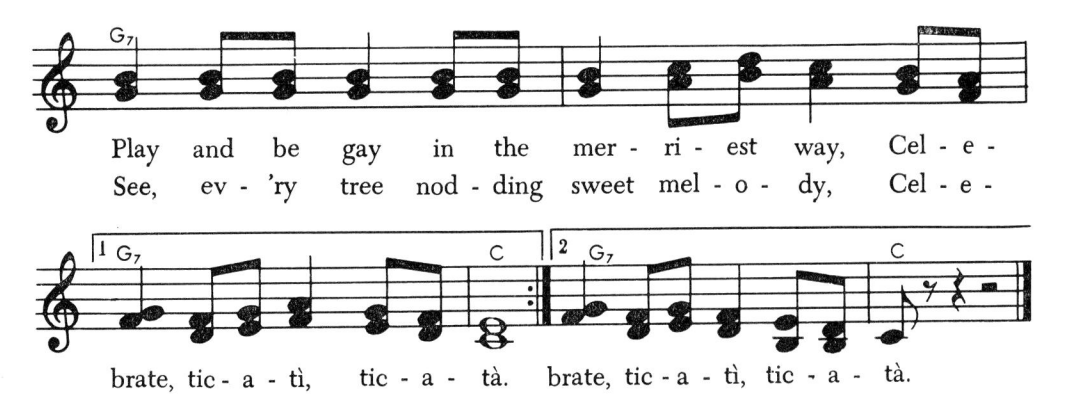

Play and be gay in the mer - ri - est way, Cel - e -
See, ev - 'ry tree nod - ding sweet mel - o - dy, Cel - e -
brate, tic - a - tì, tic - a - tà. brate, tic - a - tì, tic - a - tà.

Tic-a-tì, tic-a-tà is pronounced Tick-a-tee, tick-a-tah.

Little Burro

TRANSLATED BY ROBERTA McLAUGHLIN AND BESSIE STANCHFIELD
LATIN-AMERICAN FOLK SONG

1. Oh, now the lit - tle bur - ro Rests from all his la - bors,
2. A - diós, a - diós, Pe - ri - co, Strong he was and faith - ful,
3. Now all the folks will miss him, Hear no more his bray - ing,

He has gone to heav - en, Is mourned by all the neigh - bors.
Car - ried all his bur - dens with kicks and glan - ces bale - ful.
Loud the bell is toll - ing, And all his friends are say - ing,

Refrain
Tu - ru - ru - ru - ru - ru, Tu - ru - ru - ru - ru - ru,
Tu - ru - ru - ru - ru - ru, Tu - ru - ru - ru - ru - ru.

PROUD RIDERS

We rode hard, and brought the cattle from brushy springs,
From heavy dying thickets, leaves wet as snow;
From high places, white-grassed, and dry in the wind;
Draws where the quaken-asps were yellow and white,
And the leaves spun and spun like money spinning.
We poured them onto the trail, and rode to town.

—H. L. DAVIS

Old Texas

OKLAHOMA COWBOY SONG

1. I'm goin' to leave old Texas now,
   I'm goin' to leave old Texas now,
   They've got no use for the long-horn cow.
   They've got no use for the long-horn cow.

2. They've plowed and fenced my cattle range,
   And the people there are all so strange.

3. I'll take my horse, I'll take my rope,
   And hit the trail upon a lope.

4. Say *adios* to the Alamo
   And turn my head toward Mexico.

Night Herding Song

AMERICAN COWBOY SONG

1. Oh, slow up, do-gies, quit rov-ing a-round,
You have wan-dered and tram-pled all o-ver the ground;
Oh, graze a-long, do-gies, and feed kind-a slow,
And don't for-ev-er be on the go. Oh,
move slow, do-gies, move slow,— Hi-oo, hi-oo-oo-oo!—

2. I've cir-cle herd-ed and night herd-ed too,
But to keep you to-geth-er, that's what I can't do;
My horse is leg wear-y, and I'm aw-ful tired,
But if you get a-way, I am sure to get fired, Bunch
up, lit-tle do-gies, bunch up,— Hi-oo, hi-oo-oo-oo!—

3. Oh, lie still, dogies, since you have lain down,
Stretch away out on the big open ground;
Snore loud, little dogies, and drown the wild sound,
That will all go away, when the day rolls round,
Lie still, little dogies, lie still, Hi-oo, hi-oo-oo-oo!

Railroad Corral

AMERICAN COWBOY SONG

1. We're up in the morning ere breaking of day. The chuck wagon's busy, the flapjack's in play. The herd is a-stir over hillside and vale, With the night riders crowding them into the trail.

2. Come, take up your cinches, come shake out your reins, Come, wake your old bronco and break for the plains; Come, rout out your steers from the long chaparral, For the outfit is off to the railroad corral.

3. The sun circles upward; the steers as they plod
   Are pounding to powder the hot prairie sod;
   And it seems, as the dust makes you dizzy and sick,
   That we'll never reach noon and the cool, shady creek.

4. But tie up your kerchief and ply up your nag,
   Come dry up your grumbles and try not to lag;
   Come with your steers from the long chaparral,
   For we're far on the road to the railroad corral.

In the days following the Civil War, cattle were driven along the Chisholm and Western trails to the railroad corrals in Abilene and Dodge City, for transport to eastern markets. Such journeys took many weeks. "Chaparral" is a thicket of dwarf trees; saddles are strapped on with "cinches."

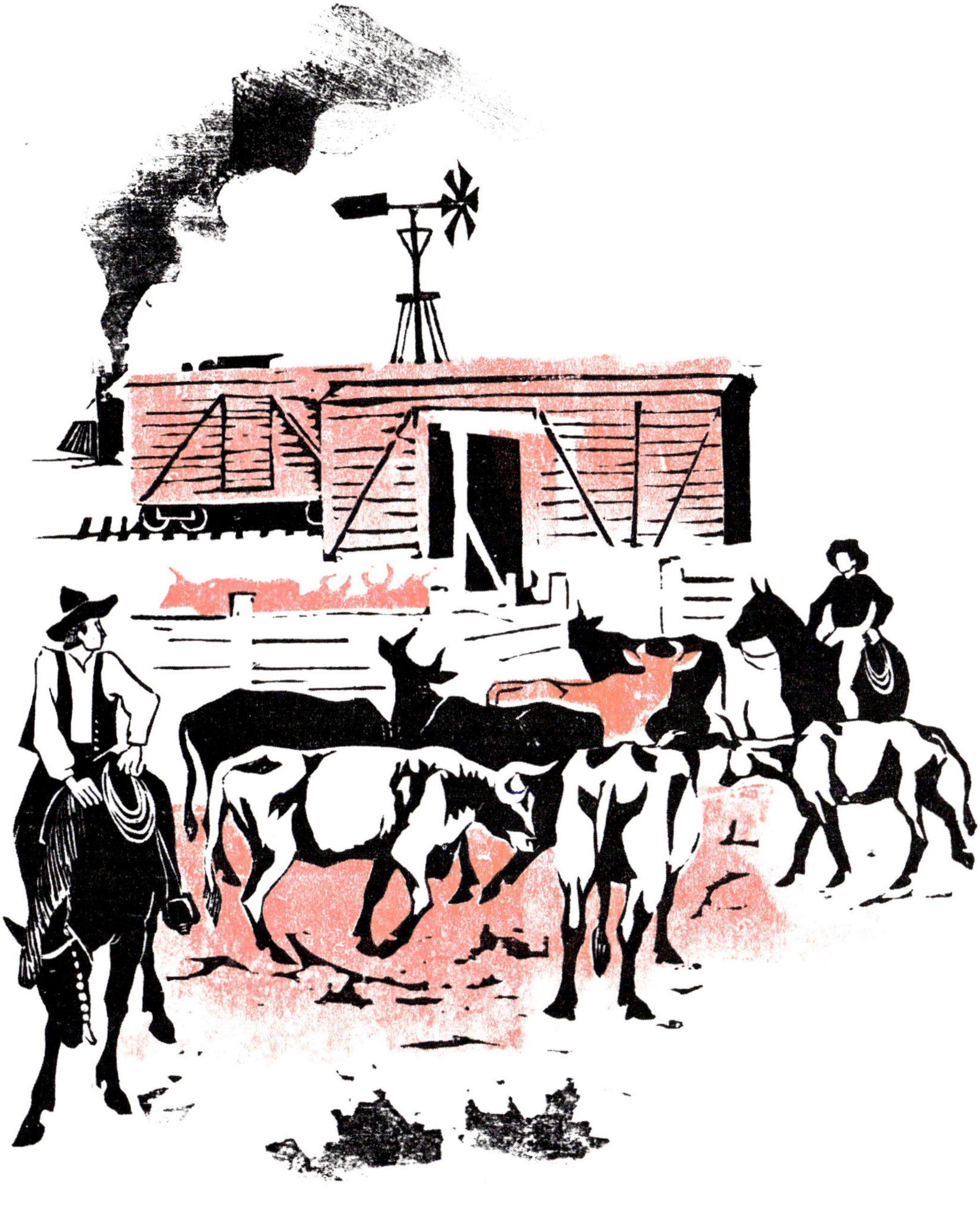

Home on the Range

AMERICAN COWBOY SONG

Here is a song with the gentle pastoral rhythm of the hills, valleys, and plains where herds and herders are at home.

1. Oh, give me a home where the buf - fa - lo roam,
2. How of - ten at night when the heav - ens are bright
3. Oh, I love those wild flowers in this dear land of ours,

Where the deer and the an - te - lope play,
With the lights from the glit - ter - ing stars,
The cur - lew I love to hear scream,

Where sel - dom is heard a dis - cour - ag - ing word,
Have I stood there a - mazed and asked as I gazed,
And I love the white rocks and the an - te - lope flocks,

And the skies are not cloud - y all day.
If their glo - ry ex - ceeds that of ours.
That graze on the moun - tain - tops green.

Refrain

Home, home on the range, Where the deer and the an - te - lope play, Where sel - dom is heard a dis - cour - ag - ing word,

And the skies are not cloud - y all day.

INSTRUMENTAL PARTS FOR THE SONG

Violins

B♭ Trumpets
B♭ Clarinets

Buffalo Gals

AMERICAN FOLK SONG

A minstrel show song, picked up by the cowboys. The minstrels sang of "Chicago gals" in Chicago and "Buffalo gals" in Buffalo. The latter title stuck.

1. As I was wan-d'ring down the street,
A pret-ty gal I chanced to meet, Oh,
Down the street, down the street,
she was fair to view.

Refrain:
Then Buf-fa-lo gals, will you come out to-night,
Will you come out to-night, will you come out to-night,
And dance by the light of the moon?

2. I stopped her an' I had some talk,
   Had some talk, had some talk,
   Her foot covered up
      the whole sidewalk,
   An' left no room for me.

3. She's the prettiest gal
      I've seen in my life,
   Seen in my life, seen in my life,
   I wish very much she was my wife,
   Then we would part no more.

Cowboys' Christmas Ball

Cowboy balls opened and closed with "Buffalo Gals"—a favorite. It was sung, danced or clapped to, and always livened the gathering.

AMERICAN COWBOY SONG

1. Way out in western Texas, where the Clear Fork's waters flow, Where the cattle are a-browsin' and the Spanish ponies grow; Where the antelope is grazin' and the lonely plovers call, It was there that I attended the cowboys' Christmas ball.

2. The music was a fiddle and a lively tambourine, And a viol came, imported by the stage from Abilene. The room was togged out gorgeous with mistletoe and shawls, And the candles flickered festious around the airy hall.

3. The leader was a feller that came from Swenson's ranch,
   They called him Windy Billy from Little Deadman's Branch,
   His rig was kinder keerless—big spurs and high-heeled boots;
   He had the reputation that comes when fellers shoot.

4. "Saloot yer lovely critters, now swing and let 'em go;
   Climb the grapevine round 'em; now all hands do-si-do;
   You maverick, jine the round-up. Now rope and balance all!"
   Hi! Hit was gettin' active, the cowboys' Christmas ball.

JOURNEYS AND ADVENTURINGS

Song of the Dawn

WORDS ANONYMOUS
MUSIC BY MILTON KAYE

In the early days of Canada the canoe train would leave at dawn, as it set out on the long voyage to distant Indian encampments. At that early hour of the day, mist lay cool and gray, low above the water. The fine particles of moisture would gather on the erect figures of the voyageurs, glistening like dust of pearls on their black beards and shining in their black hair till it seemed as if the men themselves had become a part of the wilderness. Then a voice from the leading canoe would rise from the silent river, chanting the "Song of the Dawn." Voice after voice would take it up, down the long procession of canoes, until from the last in line the chorus came, halting like an echo, through the quiet air. —Described by SIR GILBERT PARKER *in "Trail of the Sword."*

Introduction can be played throughout

Qui vive,___ Qui vive?___

Who is it cries in the dawn, Cries when the stars go down?

Who is it that comes through the mist,___ The mist that is

fine like lawn,___ The mist like an an-gel's gown?

Opening Up the Land

Who is it comes in the dawn? *Qui vive,*
Qui vive in the dawn?
Who is it passes us by, Still in the dawn and the mist?
Tall *seigneur* of the dawn, A two-edged sword at his thigh, A shield of gold at his wrist!
Who is it hurrieth by? *Qui vive,*
Qui vive in the dawn?

Mule Skinner Blues

FOLK SONG FROM SOUTHERN UNITED STATES

1. Well, it's good morn - ing, cap- tain, "Good morn- ing, son,"
And it's good morn - ing, cap- tain, "Good morn - ing son."
Do you need an - oth - er mule skin - ner
Out on your new road line?

2. Well, I like to work, I'm rolling all the time.
3. Well, it's "Hey, little water boy, Bring your wa - ter 'round."
4. Well, I'm working on that new road At a dollar and a dime a day.

Well, I like to work, I'm rolling all the time.
Well, it's "Hey, little water boy, Bring your wa - ter 'round."
Well, I'm working on that new road At a dollar and a dime day.

I can pop my in - i - tials
If you don't like your job,
Got to hang on from Monday to Saturday night.

Mule skinners were bitter rivals of the bullwhackers hired to prod ox teams over rough trails. The mules moved a wagon train faster but were very temperamental.

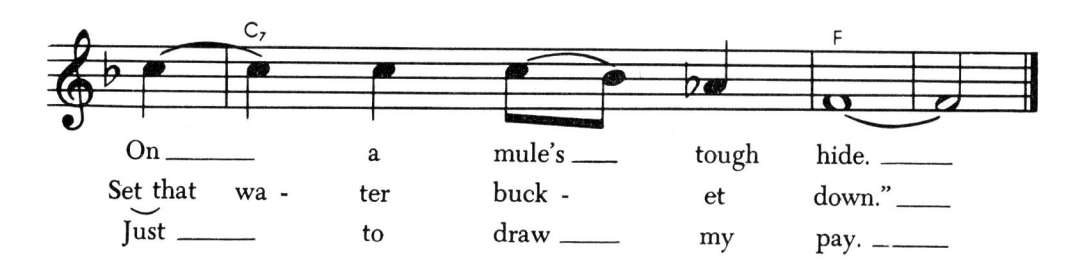

On ____ a mule's ____ tough hide. ____
Set that wa - ter buck - et down." ____
Just ____ to draw ____ my pay. ____

Push Boat

FOLK SONG FROM SOUTHERN UNITED STATES

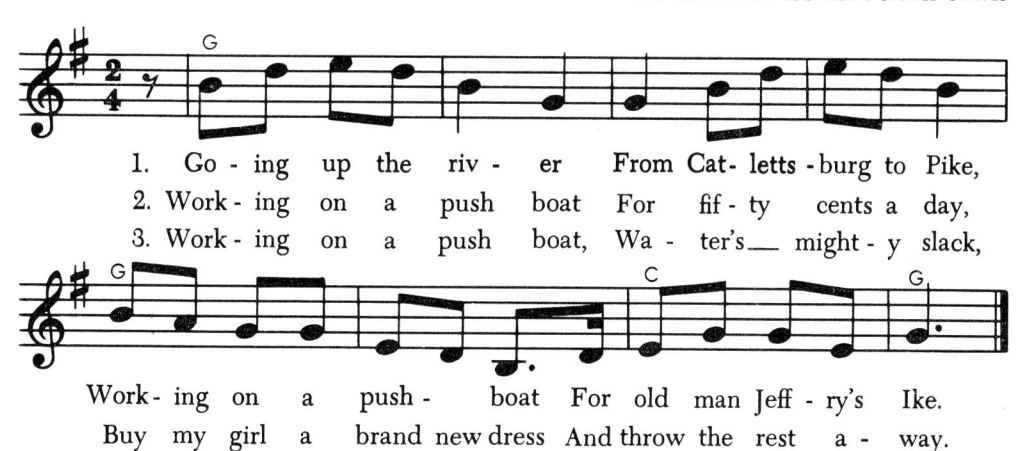

1. Go - ing up the riv - er From Cat - letts - burg to Pike,
2. Work - ing on a push boat For fif - ty cents a day,
3. Work - ing on a push boat, Wa - ter's might - y slack,

Work - ing on a push - boat For old man Jeff - ry's Ike.
Buy my girl a brand new dress And throw the rest a - way.
Tak - ing sor - ghum 'las - ses down, And bring - ing sug - ar back.

4. Pushing mighty hard, boys,
Sand bar's in the way,
Straining every muscle
To get us off today.

5. I wish I had a nickel,
I wish I had a dime,
I'd spend it all on Cynthie Jane
And dress her mighty fine.

6. The weather's mighty hot, boys,
Blisters on my feet,
Working on a push boat
To buy my bread and meat.

7. Working on a push boat,
Working in the rain,
When I get to Catlettsburg,
Good-by, Cynthie Jane.

From THE SINGIN' GATHERIN' by Jean Thomas, the "Traipsin' Woman," and Joseph A. Leeder, published by Silver Burdett Company. Reprinted by permission.

Hudson River Steamboat

FOLK SONG OF THE HUDSON RIVER VALLEY

Sand blocks play "choos" as an introduction and throughout

1. Hud-son Riv-er steam-boat, Steam-ing up and down,
2. Shad boat, pickle boat, Ly-ing side by side,
3. The "Sedge-wick" was racing and she lost all hope,

New York to Al-ba-ny Or an-y riv-er town.
Fish-er-folk and sail-or-men, Wait-ing for the tide.
Used up her steam on the big cal-li-ope,

Choo, choo to go a-head, Choo, choo to slack 'er, The
Rain cloud, storm cloud, O-ver yon-der hill,
But she hopped right a-long, She was hop-ping quick.

cap-tain and the first mate, They run the dou-ble stack-er.
Thun-der on the Dunder-berg, Rum-bles in the *kill.*
All the way from Ston-y Point to Pap-pa-lop-pen Creek.

Refrain

Choo, choo to go a-head, Choo, choo to slack 'er,

(1. & 2.) Pack-et boat, tow-boat, And a dou-ble stack-er.

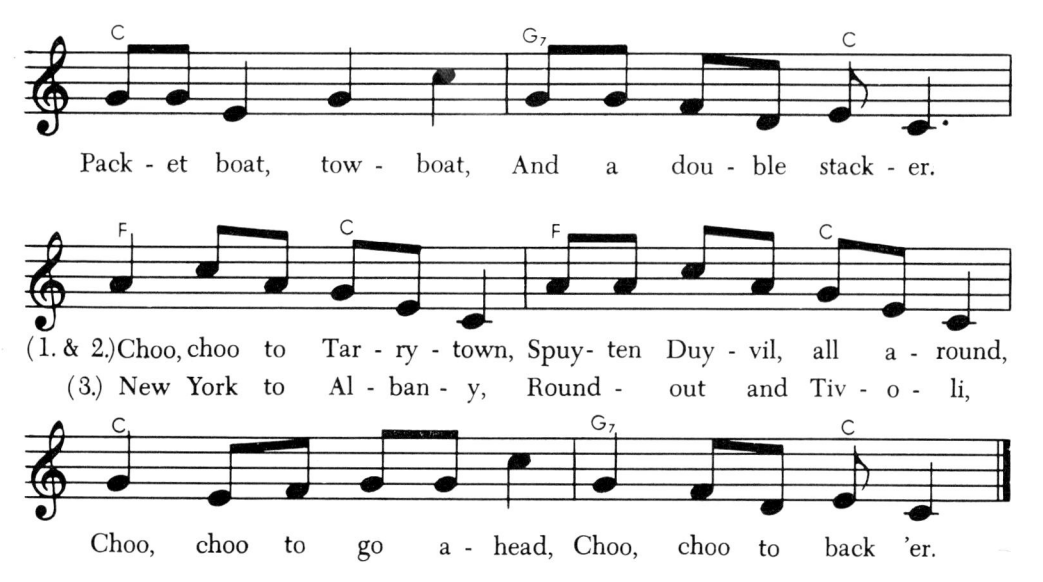

(1. & 2.) Choo, choo to Tar-ry-town, Spuy-ten Duy-vil, all a-round,
(3.) New York to Al-ban-y, Round-out and Tiv-o-li,
Choo, choo to go a-head, Choo, choo to back 'er.

The names of some of the towns and cities along the Hudson River remind us that it was the Dutch who settled in this valley. The last syllable of these names is often *kill,* the Dutch word for "stream." "Dunderberg" is one of the higher hills that flank the river. "Spuyten Duyvil" (Spy-ten Dye-vil) is the creek an early hero vowed to swim across "in spite of the devil."

The Ferry

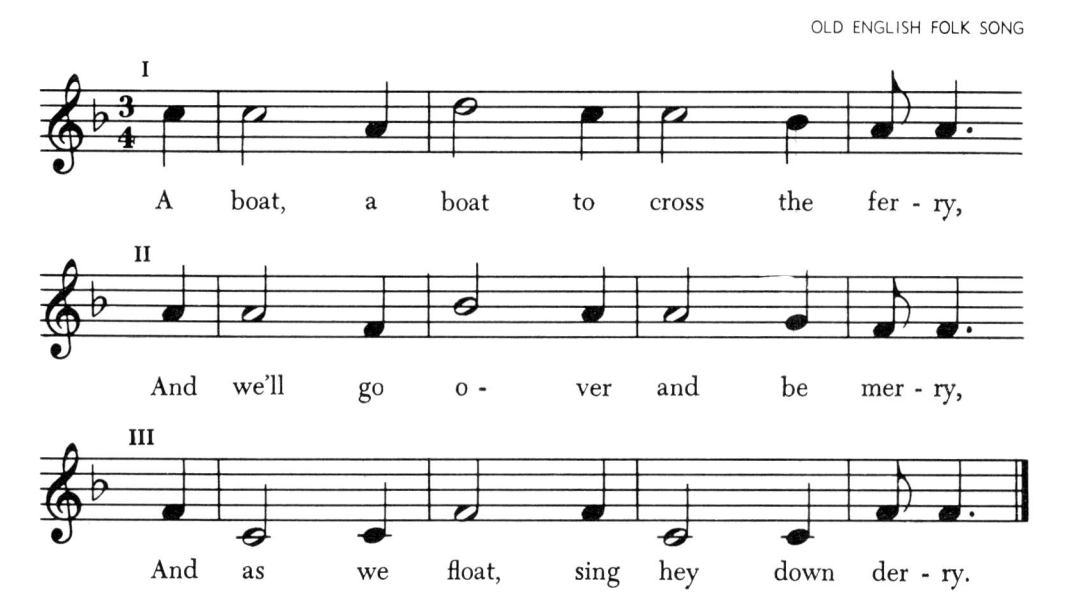

OLD ENGLISH FOLK SONG

I
A boat, a boat to cross the fer-ry,

II
And we'll go o-ver and be mer-ry,

III
And as we float, sing hey down der-ry.

Copyright, MCMXXXIII, Shawnee Press, Inc., Delaware Water Gap, Penna. Used by permission.

Don't Let Your Watch Run Down

FOLK SONG FROM TEXAS

1. Don't let your watch run down, Cap-tain, Don't let your watch run down. Work-ing on the lev-ee, dollar and a half a day, Work-ing for my Lu-lu, draw-ing my pay.

   2. Don't let your watch run down, Captain,
      Don't let your watch run down.
      Working on the railroad, mud up to my knees,
      Working for my Lulu, trying to please.

   3. Don't let your watch run down, Captain,
      Don't let your watch run down.
      When you see me coming, hoist your windows high,
      When you see me leaving, bow down and cry.

When a river overflowed, levees were built to contain it. This took hard work under a hot sun. In this song, laborers beg their boss ("Captain") to watch carefully so they don't work overtime.

Turkey in the Straw

This song went with the covered wagons across the unbroken prairies and into the Far West.

AMERICAN PIONEER SONG

1. As I was a-goin' down the road, Tired team and a heavy load, Crack my whip and the leader sprung; I says day-day to the wagon tongue.
2. Went out to milk and I didn't know how, I milked the goat instead of the cow. A monkey sittin' on a pile of straw, A-winkin' at his mother-in-law.
3. Came to the river and I couldn't get across, Paid five dollars for an old blind hoss. Wouldn't go ahead, nor he wouldn't stand still, So he went up and down like an old saw mill.

Refrain

Turkey in the straw, turkey in the hay,
Roll 'em up and twist 'em up a high tuck-a-haw,
And hit 'em up a tune called Turkey in the Straw!

Piano Chording

Erie Canal

WORK SONG OF THE ERIE CANALLERS

1. I got a mule, her name is Sal, Fif-teen miles on the E-rie Ca-nal!_ She's a good old work-er and a good old pal, Fif-teen miles on the E-rie Ca-nal!_ We've hauled some barg-es in our day, Filled with lum-ber, coal and hay, And

2. Git up there, Sal, we passed that lock, Fif-teen miles on the E-rie Ca-nal!_ And_ we'll make Rome_ 'fore_ six o'-clock, Fif-teen miles on the E-rie Ca-nal!_ Just one more trip and back we'll go Through the rain and sleet and snow, 'Cause

94

we know ev-'ry inch of the way From Al-ba-ny to Buf-fa-lo.

we know ev-'ry inch of the way From Al-ba-ny to Buf-fa-lo.

Refrain

Low bridge, ev-'ry-bod-y down, Low bridge, 'cause we're com-ing to a town, And you'll al-ways know your neigh-bor, You'll al-ways know your pal, If you ev-er nav-i-gat-ed on the E-rie Ca-nal.

95

Driving Steel

WORK SONG FROM THE DEEP SOUTH

A work song with the heavy accents and steady slow rhythm of a job that was very hard.

1. Driving steel, driving steel, driving steel, boys, is hard work, I know. Driving steel, driving steel, driving steel, boys, is hard work, I know.
2. Treat me right, treat me right, treat me right, boys, I'm bound to stay all day. Treat me wrong, treat me wrong, treat me wrong, boys, I'm bound to run away.
3. See the boss, see the boss, see the boss man a-coming down the line. See the boss, see the boss, see the boss man a-coming down the line.

A song of work gangs on the early railroad whose job it was to drive the huge steel or iron spikes through the rail bottoms into the railroad ties. Men hammered in rhythm as they sang.

Drill, Ye Tarriers

Nothing could stop the tracks being laid across the country. Rocks were blasted and mountains tunneled.

WORDS AND MUSIC BY THOMAS CASEY

1. Ev-'ry morn-ing at sev-en o'-clock There's twen-ty tar-ri-ers a-work-ing at the rock, And the boss comes a-long and he says, "Keep still, And come down heav-y on the cast iron drill."

2. Our new fore-man is Dan McCann, I'll tell you sure he's a blame mean man; Last week a prema-ture blast went off, And a mile in the air went Big Jim Goff.

3. Next time pay day comes a-round, Jim Goff was short one buck, he found; "What for?" says he; then this re-ply, "You're docked for the time you were up in the sky."

Refrain

So drill, ye tar-ri-ers, drill, And drill, ye tar-ri-ers, drill! Oh, it's work all day for sug-ar in your tay, Down be-yond the rail-way, And drill, ye tar-ri-ers, drill!

Spoken at the end: And drill! And blast! And fire!

Sis Joe

RAILROAD WORK SONG

Track Lining Holler

"When steel gets tight with the sun shinin' right warm on it, the track buck and it looks just something like an old old slavery-time fence row, in and out. Well, this day the sun was shinin', the track was buckin', and I was walkin' an' talkin'. The passenger train's due now, and I got to git out down there and line that track up straight. It's just like a knittin' needle before the passenger train gets there. I holler and call six of my best men by name. Chances are I'll call Hank Stevens, Sonny Watkin, Sam Justis, Jim Williams, to get their linin' bars and go down there. I have to tell 'em where to get it."

(spoken) FOREMAN
Go get the third johnny head and touch it north,
So the track runnin' east and west;
Touch it north!

SINGING LEADER

All right now, boys, Let me tell you 'bout Sis Joe this time.

Sis Joe,* on the M. & O., Track *heav-y* but she *will* go.

LEADER AND GANG

Take a *mule,* take a *jack,* Take a *lin-in'* bar for to *line* this track.
On the *mud* line, on the *sand,* On the *mud* line, get a *man.*
Jack the *Rabbit,* on the M. & O., Track *heav-y,* but she *will* go.

*The men heave on their lining bars on the beats indicated by the italicized words.

When you dramatize "Sis Joe," quite a group of workmen will be needed "to line the tracks." The Singing Leader will fit his lines, whenever they occur, into the first line of the printed music. (The second line of music is sung only once.) The words marked for Leader and Gang are fitted each time into the last line of music, with the italicized words falling after the measure bars.

(spoken) FOREMAN

Run on down yonder to the third johnny head and touch it easy,
Quick, make haste, I hear the train comin'.

SINGING LEADER

All right now, boys,
Let me tell you what I had for breakfast now.

LEADER AND GANG

Little *rice*, little *bean*,
No *meat* to be *seen*.

Hard *work* ain' *easy*,
Dry *bread* ain' *greasy*.

Oh, *Joe*, Joe *Lily* Butt,
Oh, *Joe*, caincha *pick* it up?

(spoken) FOREMAN

Now, wait a minute, you stop right there,
Now, put your guns on your shoulders,
And come walkin' back.
Go on to the next one and touch it just a fraction,
To the next one now and just barely move it.
I want you to just barely touch it,
Touch it just a little bit,
Just something another like a fraction.

SINGING LEADER

All right now, boys,
Let me tell you 'bout tampin' ties this time.

LEADER AND GANG

Have to *tamp* 'em up *solid*,
Have to *tamp* 'em kinda *slow*.

Jack the *Rabbit*, Jack the *Bear*,
Caincha *move* it, just a *hair*?

Sis *Joe*, don't you *hear* me now?
Sis *Joe*, don't you *hear* me now?

Continued on page 100

(spoken) FOREMAN
Now, you'll have to put your guns on your shoulders an' come by me,
An' come in a hurry,
Come trottin',
Come laughin',
Come like you gonna get paid for it,
Get a move on you,
An' go by the water tank and get you some water.
Git your linin' bars an' git your backbreakin' holts,
Throw it north.

LEADER AND GANG

Yea,— oh, *yea,*
Yea,— oh, *yea,*

In the *mornin'* when you *rise,*
Pick and *shevil* by your *side.*

In the *mornin'* when you *rise,*
Got a *pain* in your *side.*

(spoken) FOREMAN
Now, boys, put yo' guns on yo' shoulders an' get back in the shade.

Wabash Cannon Ball

WORDS AND MUSIC BY WILLIAM KINDT

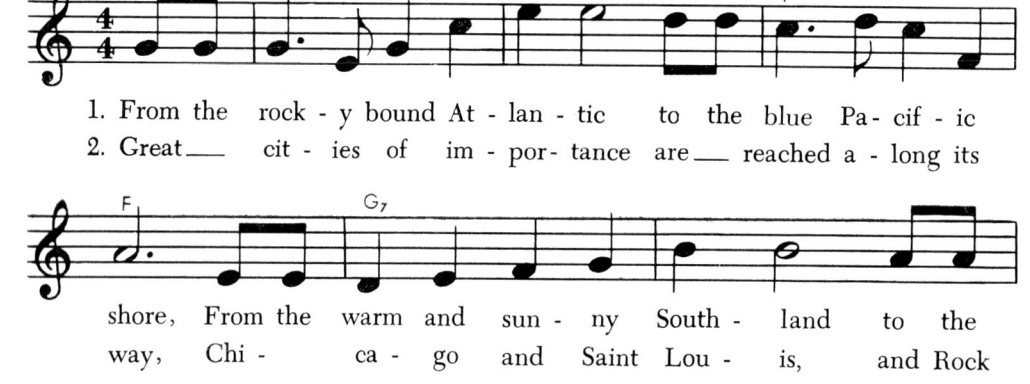

1. From the rock-y bound At-lan-tic to the blue Pa-cif-ic shore, From the warm and sun-ny South-land to the
2. Great cit-ies of im-por-tance are reached a-long its way, Chi-ca-go and Saint Lou-is, and Rock

isle of La - bra - dor, There's a name of mag - ic
Is - land so they say, And Spring - field and De -
splen - dor that is known quite well to all, 'Tis the
ca - tur, and Pe - or - ia, last of all, 'Tis the
won - drous com - bi - na - tion called the WA - BASH CAN - NON BALL,
west - ern ter - mi - na - tion of the WA - BASH CAN - NON BALL.

Refrain

Then lis - ten to the jin - gle, the rum - ble, and the roar
Of the might - y rush - ing en - gine as she
streams a - long the shore, Hear the thun - der on the
steel rails, hear the bell and whis - tle call, As you
roll a - long in safe - ty on the WA - BASH CAN - NON BALL.

Mingo Mountain

KENTUCKY MOUNTAIN SONG

Tablature for Guitar

Melody

1. I've been trav-'ling o-ver these moun-tains For-ty long years, for-ty long years. I'm going back to the Min-go Moun-tains, That's my home, That's my home, That's my home.
2. There's no ham-mer on these moun-tains Rings like mine, rings like mine. This old ham-mer rings like sil-ver, Shines like gold, Shines like gold, Shines like gold.

Yes, for-ty long years.
Yes, rings like mine.

102

*I'm going to sit on the long green bench
Where the old sea captains talk;
The wind is rising,
The glass is falling,
The gulls are calling,
And nobody wants to talk!*
—AGNES LOUISE DEAN

Mississippi Sounding Calls

CALLS OF MISSISSIPPI RIVERBOAT PILOTS

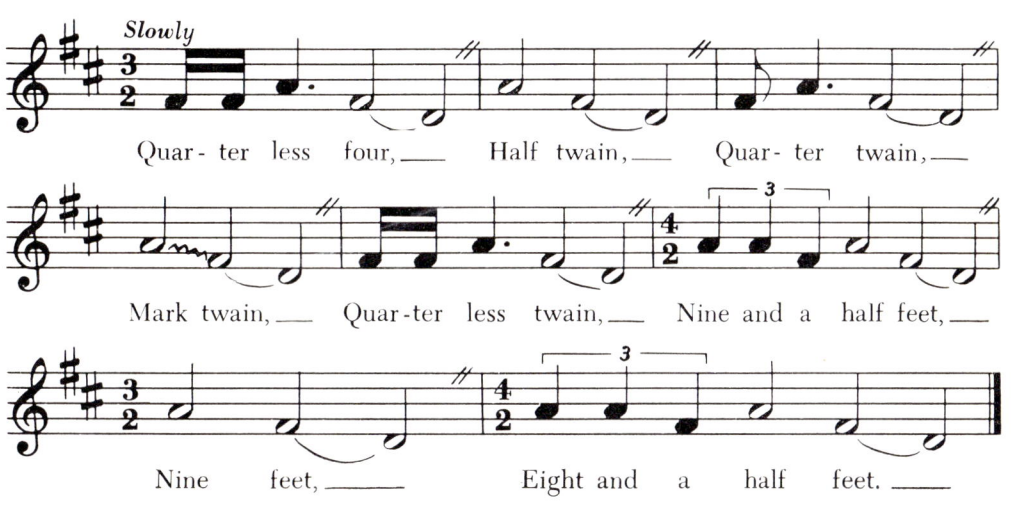

Quar-ter less four,___ Half twain,___ Quar-ter twain,___
Mark twain,___ Quar-ter less twain,___ Nine and a half feet,___
Nine feet,___ Eight and a half feet.___

The job of the "sounding man" stationed on the prows of Mississippi paddle-wheelers was to keep the boat from getting stuck on a sandbar. "Mark twain" (two fathoms) inspired a well-known nom de plume.

The Forty-Niners
Santy Anno

Gold was discovered in California in 1848. By 1849 the rush was underway. Cross-country travel was still slow and hard; many sailed around Cape Horn.

SEA CHANTEY

1. We're sailing down the river from Liverpool,
   Heave away, Santy Anno;
   Around Cape Horn to Frisco Bay,
   All on the plains of Mexico.

   Refrain:
   So heave her up and away we'll go,
   Heave away, Santy Anno,
   Heave her up and away we'll go,
   All on the plains of Mexico.

2. She's a fast clipper ship and a bully good crew,
   Heave away, Santy Anno;
   A down-East Yankee for her captain, too.
   All on the plains of Mexico.

3. There's plenty of gold,
      so I've been told,
   Heave away, Santy Anno;
   There's plenty of gold,
      so I've been told,
   Way out west to Californio.

4. Back in the days
      of Forty-nine,
   Heave away, Santy Anno;
   Those are the days
      of the good old times,
   All on the plains of Mexico.

The California gold rush drew people from all over the world. The population of this territory increased so fast that in 1850 it was admitted as a state.

Sacramento

WORDS TRADITIONAL
MUSIC BY STEPHEN FOSTER

1. We've formed our band and we are well manned, Doo-da, doo-da!
To jour-ney a-far to the Prom-ised Land, Doo-da, doo-da, day!

2. Where the gold-en ore is rich in store,
On the banks of the Sac-ra-men-to shore,

Refrain
Blow, boys, blow, To Cal-i-for-nia go!
There's plen-ty of gold, so I've been told,
On the banks of the Sac-ra-men-to!

3. As the gold is thar most any whar,
   And they dig it out with an iron bar,
   Blow, boys, blow, to California go!
   There's plenty of gold, so I've been told,
   On the banks of the Sacramento!

4. And whar 'tis thick, with a spade or pick,
   They can take out lumps as heavy as a brick.
   Blow, boys, blow, to California go!
   There's plenty of gold, so I've been told,
   On the banks of the Sacramento!

Eight Bells

SEA CHANTEY

It was a long voyage around Cape Horn. Story-telling songs helped keep sailors amused.

1. My husband's a saucy foretopman, A chum of the cook's don't you know,— He put his head down the cook's funnel, And shouted, "Come up from below!"—
2. My husband once shipped in a whaler, And sailed to the far northern seas,— But being a bold-hearted sailor, He cared not for ice, sea, nor breeze.—
3. And now he's no longer a sailor, He often wakes up in the night,— And thinking he's still on the whaler, Cries out with the greatest delight:—

Refrain

Eight bells!— Eight bells!— Rouse out there the watch from below!— Eight bells!— Eight bells!— Rouse out there the watch from below!—

When the day watch on a sailing vessel had eaten the evening meal, the men gathered on the small upper deck before the mast, called the forecastle, to relax by singing songs and playing instruments. Whereas sea chanteys are songs which helped men to work in rhythm, forecastle songs were to amuse.

Clementine

This silly song developed in San Francisco, an obvious outgrowth of the hectic days of forty-nine.

AMERICAN FOLK SONG

1. In a cavern, in a canyon, Excavating for a mine, Dwelt a miner, forty-niner, And his daughter, Clementine.

2. Light she was, and like a fairy, And her shoes were number nine, Herring boxes without topses, Sandals were for Clementine.

Refrain:
O my darling, O my darling, O my darling Clementine! You are lost and gone forever, Dreadful sorry, Clementine!

3. Drove she ducklings to the water
   Every morning just at nine,
   Hit her foot against a splinter,
   Fell into the foaming brine.

4. Then the miner, forty-niner,
   Soon began to peak and pine,
   Thought he oughter jine his daughter,
   Now he's with his Clementine.

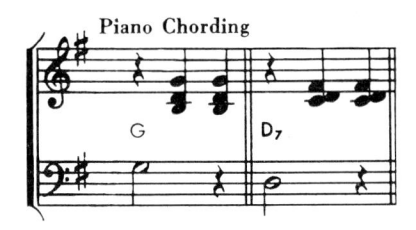

Piano Chording

Song of the Fishes

WORDS ADAPTED BY BURL IVES
FORECASTLE FISHING SONG

1. Come all ye bold fisher-men, listen to me,
   I'll sing you a song of the fish in the sea.
2. First comes the blue fish a-wagging his tail,
   He comes up on deck and yells, "All hands make sail!"

Refrain

So blow, blow, westerly blow,
So blow, ye winds, westerly, westerly blow,—
We're bound southward, Steady we go.
We're bound to the southward, so steady we go.

3. Next come the eels with their nimble tails,
   They jumped up aloft and loosed all the sails.

4. Next come the herrings with their little tails,
   They manned sheets and halyards and set all the sails.

5. Next comes the porpoise with his short snout,
   He jumps on the bridge and yells: "Ready, about!"

6. Next comes the swordfish, the scourge of the sea,
   The order he gives is: "Helm's a-lee!"

7. Then comes the turbot, as red as a beet,
   He shouts from the bridge: "Stick out that foresheet!"

8. Having accomplished these wonderful feats,
   The blackfish sings out next to: "Rise tacks and sheets!"

9. Next comes the whale, the largest of all,
   Singing out from the bridge: "Haul taut, mainsail, haul!"

10. Then comes the mackerel with his striped back,
    He flopped on the bridge and yelled: "Board the main tack!"

11. Next comes the sprat, the smallest of all,
    He sings out: "Haul well taut, let go and haul!"

12. Along comes the dolphin, flapping his tail,
    He yelled to the boatswain to reef the foresail.

13. Up jumps the fisherman, stalwart and grim,
    And with his big net he scoops them all in.

Shenandoah

SEA CHANTEY

1. Oh, Shen-an-doah, I long to hear you,
   A-way, you roll-ing riv-er.
2. I long to see your smil-ing val-ley,
   Oh, Shen-an-doah, I long to hear you,
   I long to see your smil-ing val-ley,
   A-way, I'm bound a-way, 'Cross the wide Mis-sou-ri.

3. Oh, Shenandoah, I'm bound to leave you,
   Oh, Shenandoah, I'll not deceive you.

4. Oh, Shenandoah, I long to hear you,
   Oh, Shenandoah, I long to hear you.

Into the West

The Promised Land

WHITE SPIRITUAL

Across the Great Plains rolled the covered wagon trains! New settlers sang this song about "the promised land."

1. On Jordan's stormy banks I stand And cast a wishful eye To Canaan's fair and happy land Where my possessions lie.
2. There gen-'rous fruits that never fail On trees immortal grow; There rocks and hills and brooks and vales With milk and honey flow.
3. Oh, the transporting rap-t'rous scene That rises to my sight, Sweet fields arrayed in living green And rivers in delight.

Refrain

I am bound for the promised land, Bound for the promised land. Oh, who will come and go with me? I am bound for the promised land.

The wagon trains freighting supplies to settlers traveled fifteen miles a day when a bullwhacker goaded the oxen with a long whip.

Bullwhacker's Epic

FOLK SONG FROM WESTERN UNITED STATES

1. Oh, I'm a jolly bull-whack-er on the Salt Lake Cit-y Line, And I can lick the ras-cal that yokes an ox of mine. He'd bet-ter turn him out or you bet your life I'll try To sprawl him with an ox-bow Root hog, or die.

2. It's out on the road with a ver-y heav-y load, With a ver-y awk-ward team And a ver-y mud-dy road, You may crack the whip and hol-ler, You may push and pull and pry, But whack the cat-tle on, boys, Root hog, or die.

3. It's out on the road
   These sights are to be seen,
   The antelopes and buffalo,
   The prairie all so green,
   The antelopes and buffalo,
   The rabbit jumps so high;
   It's whack the cattle on, boys,
   Root hog or die.

4. It's every day at twelve
   There's something for to do;
   And if there's nothing else,
   There's a pony for to shoe;
   I'll throw him down,
   And still I'll make him lie;
   Little pig, big pig,
   Root hog or die.

O Susanna

WORDS AND MUSIC BY STEPHEN FOSTER

Journeying by covered wagon was tedious, hard, and slow. This song was taken along to break the monotony.

1. I came from Alabama With my banjo on my knee,
I'm going to Louisiana, My true love for to see;
It rained all night the day I left, The weather it was dry;
The sun so hot I froze to death; Susanna, don't you cry.

2. I had a dream the other night, When ev'rything was still.
I thought I saw Susanna A-coming down the hill.
The buckwheat cake was in her mouth, The tear was in her eye.
Says I, "I'm coming from the South, Susanna, don't you cry."

Refrain
Oh, Susanna, Oh, don't you cry for me,
I've come from Alabama With my banjo on my knee.

Piano Chording

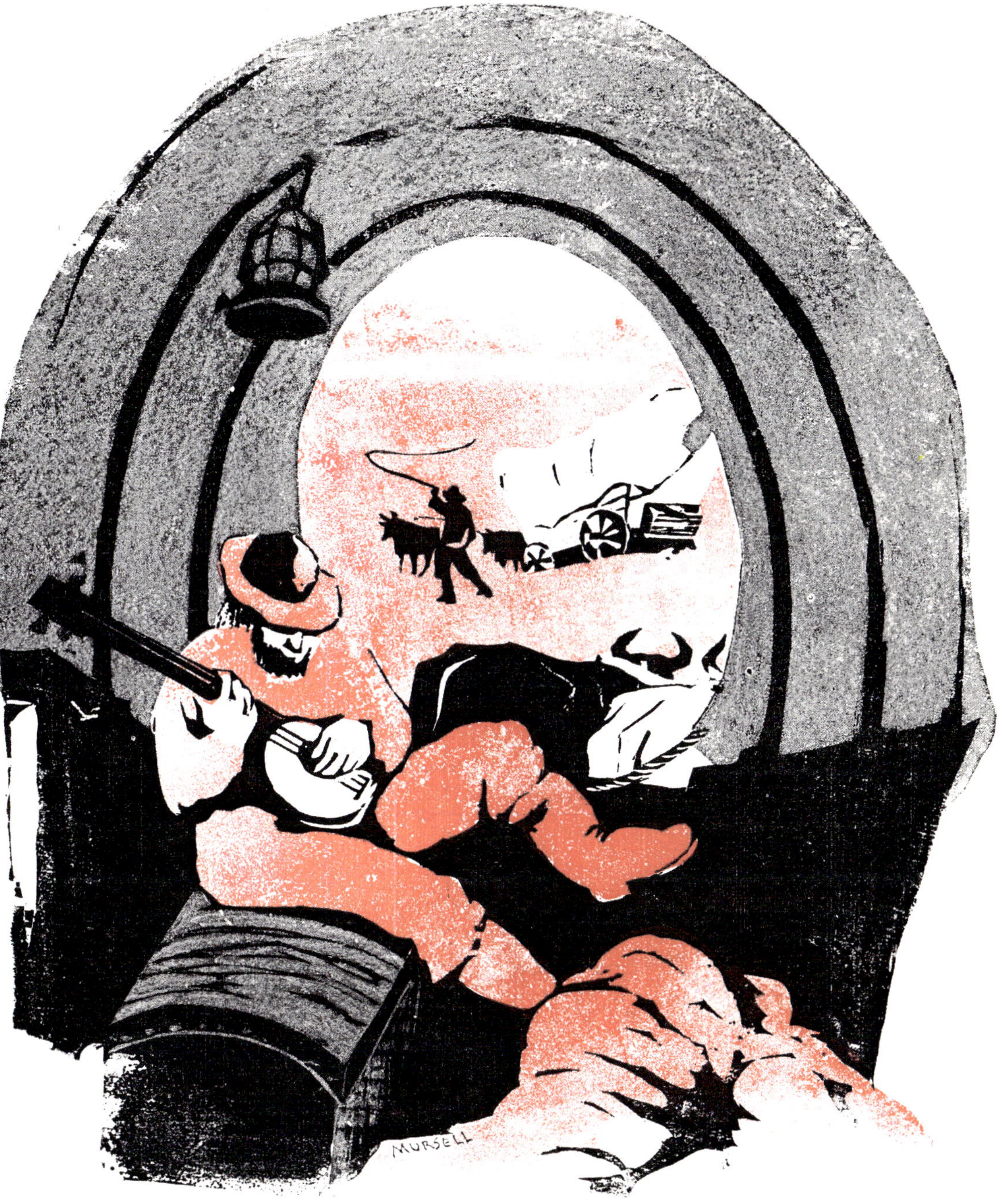
MURSELL

BUFFALO DUSK

The buffaloes are gone.
And those who saw the buffaloes are gone.
Those who saw the buffaloes by thousands and how they pawed the
  prairie sod into dust with their hoofs, their great
  heads down pawing on in the great pageant of dusk,
Those who saw the buffaloes are gone.
And the buffaloes are gone.
  —CARL SANDBURG

Shoot the Buffalo

PLAY-PARTY SONG FROM OKLAHOMA

1. Rise you up, my dear-est dear, and pre-sent to me your hand,
   We are roam-ing in suc-ces-sion to some far and dis-tant land,
   To some far and dis-tant land, to some far and dis-tant land,
   We are roam-ing in suc-ces-sion to some far and dis-tant land.

2. Oh, the buf-fa-lo is dead, for we shot him in the head;
   We will ral-ly round the cane-brake, And we'll shoot the buf-fa-lo.
   And we'll shoot the buf-fa-lo, and we'll shoot the buf-fa-lo,
   We will ral-ly round the cane-brake, and we'll shoot the buf-fa-lo.

Great-Granddad

AMERICAN COWBOY SONG

1. Great-granddad, when the land was young,
   Barred the door with a wagon tongue,
   For the times was rough and the redskins mocked,
   And he said his prayers with his shotgun cocked.

2. He was a citizen tough and grim,
   Danger was duck soup to him.
   He ate corn pone and bacon fat,
   Great-grandson would starve on that.

3. Great-granddad was a busy man;
   Cooked his grub in a frying pan.
   He picked his teeth with his hunting knife,
   He wore the same suit all of his life.

4. Twenty-one children came to bless
   The old man's house in the wilderness.
   But great-granddad didn't lose heart,
   The boys hunted rabbits and they ketched right smart.

5. Twenty-one boys and how they grew,
   Tall and strong on the bacon, too.
   Slept on the floor with the dogs and cats,
   And hunted in the woods in their coonskin caps.

From the songbook THE COWBOY SINGS, edited by Kenneth S. Clark. Copyright MCMXXXII, Shawnee Press, Inc., Delaware Water Gap, Pennsylvania. Used by permission.

The Railroad Cars Are Coming

WORK SONG OF THE RAILROAD GANGS

1. The great Pacific railway, For California hail!
   Bring on the locomotive, Lay down the iron rail;
   Across the rolling prairies, By steam we're bound to go,

2. The little dogs in dogtown Will wag each little tail;
   They'll think that something's coming A-riding on a rail.
   The rattlesnake shows its fangs, — The owl tu-whit tu-whoo.

Refrain

The railroad cars are coming, humming Through New Mexico, The railroad cars are coming, humming Through New Mexico.

"The little dogs in dogtown" is a reference to the prairie dogs that abounded at that time.

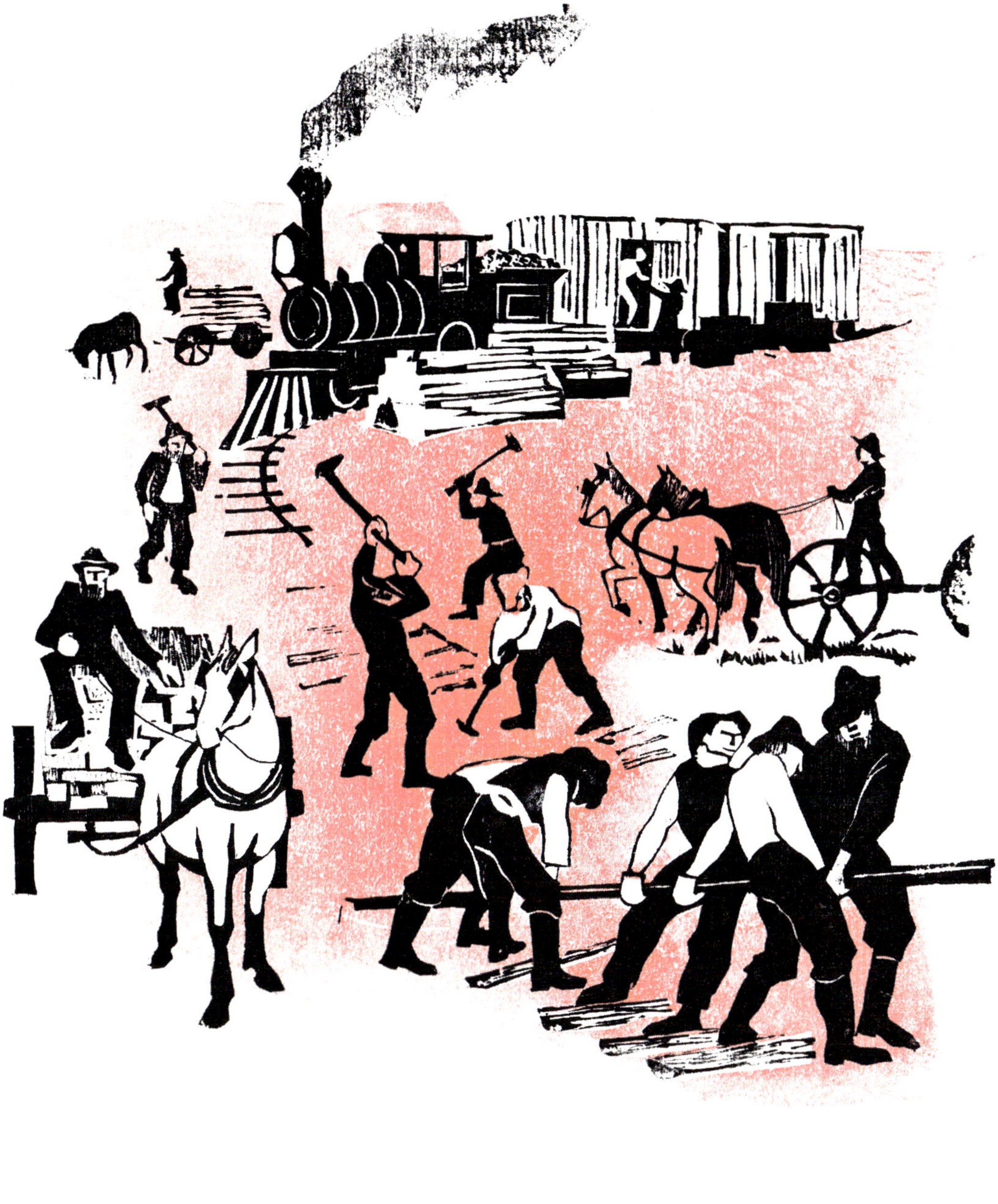

The Little Old Sod Shanty

FOLK SONG FROM THE WESTERN PLAINS

1. I am look-ing rath-er seed-y now while hold-ing down my claim,
And my vict-uals are not al-ways of the best.
And the mice play shy-ly round me as I nes-tle down to rest,
In my lit-tle old sod shan-ty in the West.

2. Yet I rath-er like the nov-el-ty of liv-ing in this way,
Though my bill of fare is al-ways rath-er tame;
But I'm hap-py as a clam on the land of Un-cle Sam,
In my lit-tle old sod shan-ty on my claim.

Refrain

Oh, the hing-es are of leath-er and the win-dows have no glass,
While the board roof lets the howl-ing bliz-zards in.
And I hear the hun-gry coy-ote as he slinks up through the grass,

Round my lit-tle old sod shan-ty on my claim.

Old Chisholm Trail

AMERICAN COWBOY SONG

The western cattle industry began in Texas before the covered wagon days. The "long drive" to market came later, as Eastern cities grew, and there was a demand for meat.

1. Come a-long, boys, and lis-ten to my tale, I'll tell you of my trou-bles on the old Chis-holm Trail,
2. Start-ed up the trail Oc-to-ber twen-ty-third, I start-ed up the trail with the 2-U herd,

Refrain
Com-a-ti yi you-py you-py yay, you-py yay,
Com-a-ti yi you-py you-py yay.

3. Oh, a ten-dollar hoss and a forty-dollar saddle,
And I'm goin' to punchin' Texas cattle.

4. I woke up one morning on the old Chisholm Trail,
Rope in my hand and a cow by the tail.

5. I'm up in the mornin' afore daylight,
And afore I sleep the moon shines bright.

Utah Iron Horse

MORMON SONG
WORDS AND MUSIC ADAPTED BY BURL IVES

1. The I-ron Horse draws nigh With its smoke nos-trils high,
Eat-ing fire while he graz-eth, Drink-ing wa-ter while he blaz-eth;
Then the steam for-ces out, Whis-tles loud clear the route,
For the I-ron Horse is com-ing with a train in his wake.

2. If alive we shall be,
Many folks we shall see,
Nobles, lords, flotsam, beggars,
Among us will come the slavers.
Saints will come, sinners too.
We'll have all that we can do,
For this great Union Railroad
It will fetch the people through.

Work on the cross-country railroad commissioned by Congress in 1862 began on both ends, eastward from the West Coast and westward from Omaha. Intense rivalry kept both road gangs laying track at a good clip. The two met in Salt Lake City, Utah, in 1869. Two locomotives, one from each end, met amid great ceremony and the last spike in this Union Pacific Railroad was driven. It was made of solid gold. The crowd the Mormons dreaded in this song was there—to celebrate!

OUR ENDURING MEMORIES

A. D. 1620

EDWARD MACDOWELL

The Mayflower rides the waves

The Pilgrim's song of faith

121

America

WORDS BY SAMUEL FRANCIS SMITH
MUSIC BY HENRY CAREY

1. My country! 'tis of thee, Sweet land of liberty,
   Of thee I sing; Land where my fathers died,
   Land of the Pilgrim's pride, From ev'ry
   mountain side Let freedom ring.

2. My native country, thee, Land of the noble free,
   Thy name I love; I love thy rocks and rills,
   Thy woods and templed hills, My heart with
   rapture thrills Like that above.

3. Let music swell the breeze, And ring from all the trees
   Sweet Freedom's song; Let mortal tongues awake,
   Let all that breathe partake, Let rocks their
   silence break, The sound prolong.

4. Our fathers' God, to Thee,
   Author of liberty,
   To Thee we sing.
   Long may our land be bright
   With freedom's holy light;
   Protect us by Thy might,
   Great God, our King!

INSTRUMENTAL PARTS FOR THE SONG

Three Little Ships

WORDS BY NANCY NORWOOD
MUSIC BY HOAGY CARMICHAEL

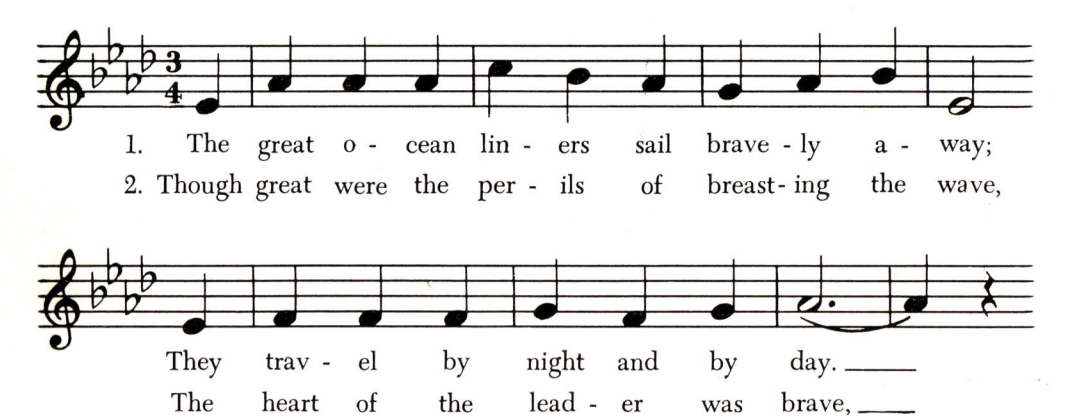

1. The great o-cean lin-ers sail brave-ly a-way;
2. Though great were the per-ils of breast-ing the wave,

They trav-el by night and by day.
The heart of the lead-er was brave,

But brav - er than these were the ven - ture - some three,
His faith nev - er failed as they bat - tled the sea,
The *Pin - ta,* the *Ni - ña,* the *San - ta Ma - rie.*
The *Pin - ta,* the *Ni - ña,* the *San - ta Ma - rie.*

They had no en - gines to pull them through gales,
You o - cean lin - ers that jour - ney with pride,
They trav - eled by gath - er - ing wind in their sails.
Re - mem - ber who first crossed the o - cean so wide:

Co - lum - bus was proud as he gazed at the three,
Co - lum - bus so brave and his ven - ture - some three,
The *Pin - ta,* the *Ni - ña,* the *San - ta Ma - rie.*
The *Pin - ta,* the *Ni - ña,* the *San - ta Ma - rie.*

Yankee Doodle

WORDS BY DR. SHACKBURG
MUSIC TRADITIONAL

The British made this song to poke fun at the ragged "Yankee" troops that came to help them fight the French and Indians.

1. Fath'r and I went down to camp, A-long with Cap-tain Good-in', And there we saw the men and boys As thick as has-ty pud-din'.
2. And there we see a thou-sand men, As rich as Squire Da-vid; And what they wast-ed ev-'ry day, I wish it could be sav-ed.

Refrain

Yan-kee Doo-dle keep it up, Yan-kee Doo-dle dan-dy, Mind the mu-sic and the step, And with the girls be han-dy.

3. And there was Captain Washington
   Upon a slapping stallion,
   A-giving orders to his men;
   I guess there was a million.

4. And then the feathers on his head,
   They look'd so very fine, ah!
   I wanted peskily to get
   To give to my Jemima.

5. And there I see a swamping gun,
   Large as a log of maple,
   Upon a mighty little cart;
   A load for father's cattle.

6. And every time they fired it off,
   It took a horn of powder;
   It made a noise like father's gun
   Only a nation louder.

7. And there I see a little keg,
   Its head all made of leather,
   They knocked upon't with little sticks,
   To call the folks together.

8. And Cap'n Davis had a gun,
   He kind o'clapt his hand on't
   And stuck a crooked stabbing-iron
   Upon the little end on't.

9. The troopers, too, would gallop up
   And fire right in our faces;
   It scared me almost half to death
   To see them run such races.

10. It scared me so I hooked it off,
    Nor stopped, as I remember,
    Nor turned about till I got home,
    Locked up in mother's chamber.

Johnny Has Gone for a Soldier

SONG OF THE AMERICAN REVOLUTION

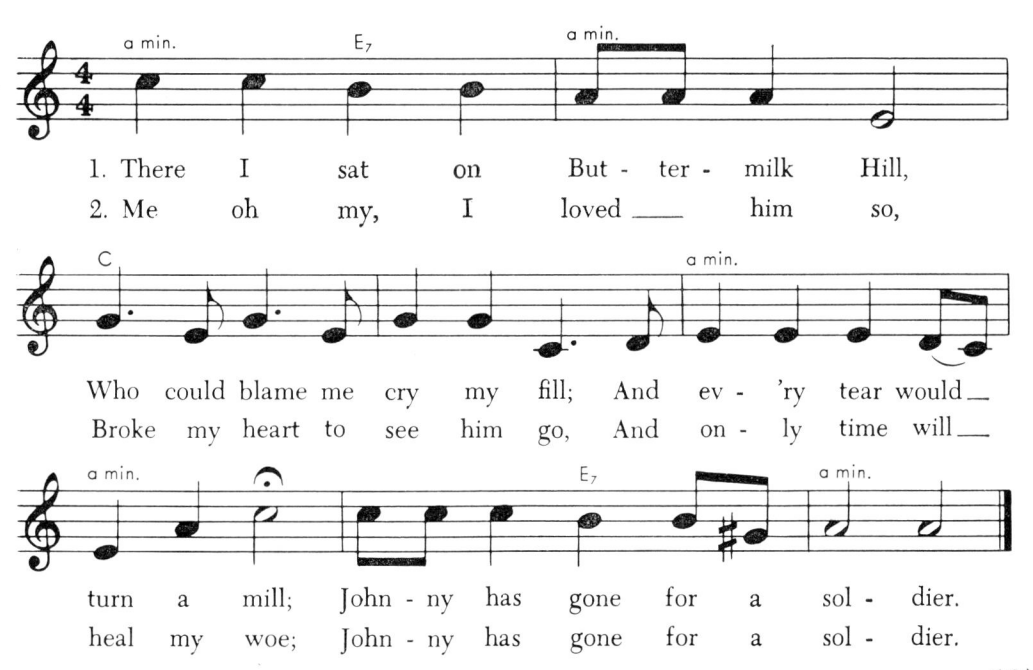

1. There I sat on Buttermilk Hill,
   Who could blame me cry my fill;
   And ev'ry tear would turn a mill;
   Johnny has gone for a soldier.

2. Me oh my, I loved him so,
   Broke my heart to see him go,
   And only time will heal my woe;
   Johnny has gone for a soldier.

Riflemen of Bennington

SONG OF THE AMERICAN REVOLUTION

Why come ye hith-er, Red-coats, your mind what mad-ness fills?
In our val-leys there is dan-ger, and there's dan-ger on our hills! Oh, hear ye not the sing-ing of the bu-gle, wild and free? Full soon you'll know the ring-ing of the ri-fle from the tree. For the ri-fle, (Clap) For the ri-fle, (Clap) in our hands, will prove no tri-fle.

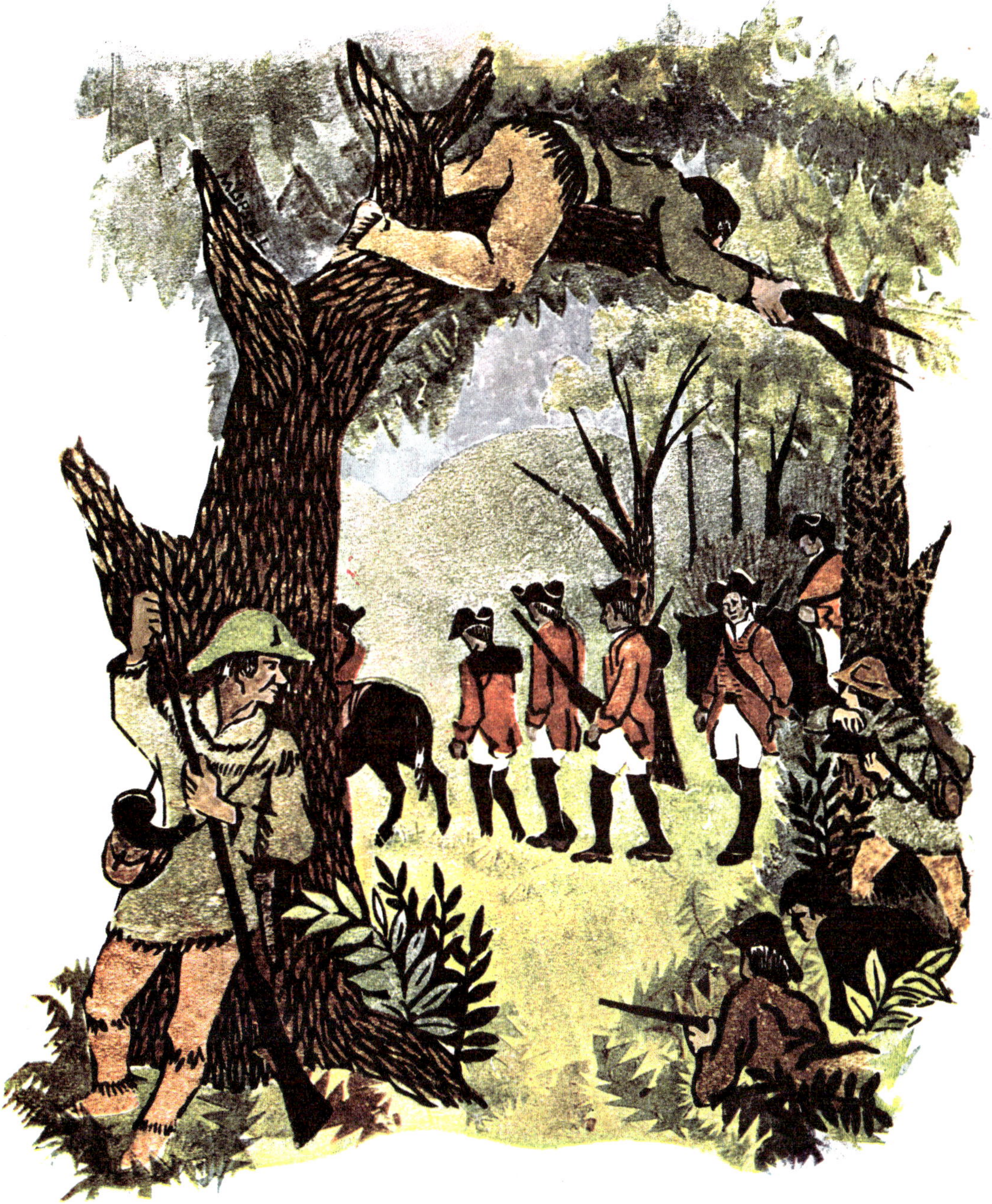

The Star-Spangled Banner

WORDS BY FRANCIS SCOTT KEY
MUSIC BY JOHN STAFFORD SMITH

1. Oh, say! can you see, by the dawn's early light,
What so proudly we hailed at the twilight's last gleaming?
Whose broad stripes and bright stars, through the perilous fight,
O'er the ramparts we watched were so gallantly streaming?
And the rockets' red glare, the bombs bursting in air,
Gave proof through the night that our flag was still there.

2. On the shore, dimly seen through the mists of the deep,
Where the foe's haughty host in dread silence reposes,
What is that which the breeze, o'er the towering steep,
As it fitfully blows, half conceals, half discloses?
Now it catches the gleam of the morning's first beam,
In full glory reflected now shines on the stream;

3. Oh, thus be it ever when free men shall stand
Between their loved homes and the war's desolation!
Blest with vict'ry and peace, may the heav'n-rescued land
Praise the Pow'r that hath made and preserved us a nation!
Then conquer we must, for our cause it is just,
And this be our motto: "In God is our trust!"

Refrain

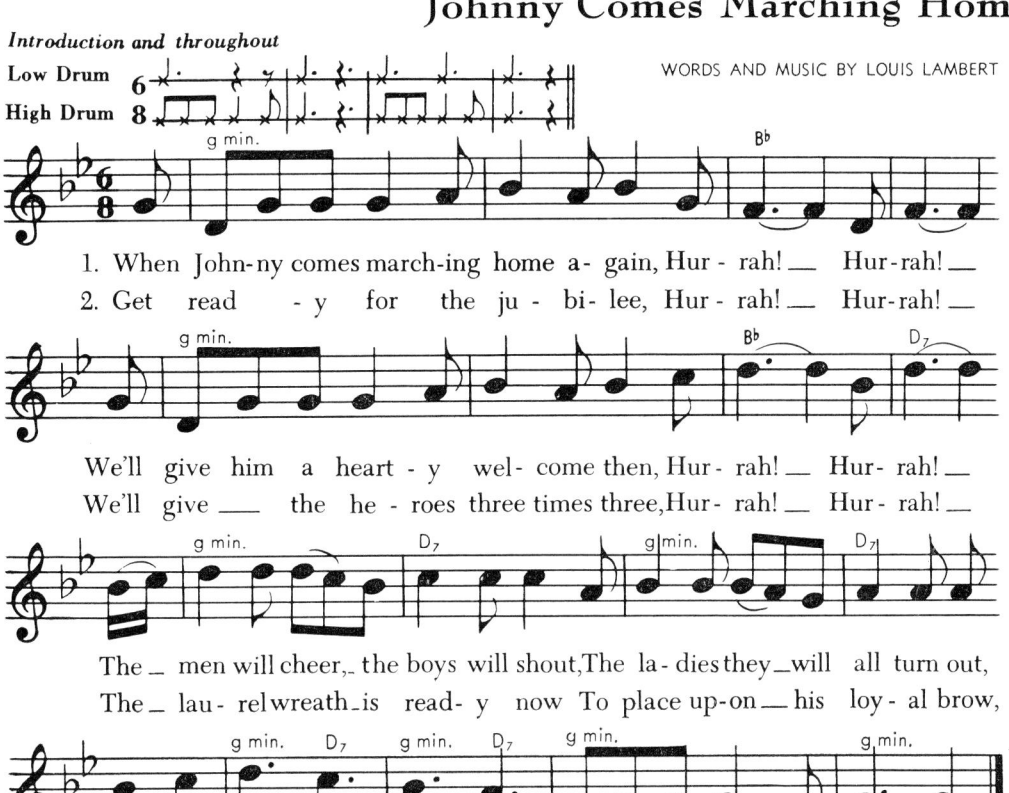

Oh, say, does that Star-Spangled Banner yet wave
'Tis the Star-Spangled Banner, oh, long may it wave
And the Star-Spangled Banner in triumph shall wave
O'er the land of the free and the home of the brave.

Johnny Comes Marching Home

WORDS AND MUSIC BY LOUIS LAMBERT

Introduction and throughout
Low Drum / High Drum

1. When Johnny comes marching home again, Hurrah! Hurrah!
2. Get ready for the jubilee, Hurrah! Hurrah!

We'll give him a hearty welcome then, Hurrah! Hurrah!
We'll give the heroes three times three, Hurrah! Hurrah!

The men will cheer, the boys will shout, The ladies they will all turn out,
The laurel wreath is ready now To place upon his loyal brow,

And we'll all feel gay When Johnny comes marching home!
And we'll all feel gay When Johnny comes marching home!

131

Dixie

WORDS AND MUSIC BY DAN D EMMETT

1. I wish I was in the land of cot-ton, Old times there are not for-got-ten, Look a-way! Look a-way! Look a-way! Dix-ie Land. In Dix-ie Land where I was born in, Ear-ly on one frost-y morn-in' Look a-way, look a-way, look a-way, Dix-ie Land!

2. There's buck-wheat cakes and In-dian bat-ter, Makes you fat or a lit-tle fat-ter, Look a-way! Look a-way! Look a-way! Dix-ie Land. Then hoe it down and scratch your grab-ble, To Dix-ie Land I'm bound to trav-el, Look a-way, look a-way, look a-way, Dix-ie Land!

132

The banjo was invented in Dixie. Your guitar can sound like a banjo if you strum it with pick very close to the bridge. Also strum on the higher-pitched strings on your autoharp, using brisk strokes, to simulate banjo.

Refrain

Then I wish I was in Dix-ie, hoo-ray, hoo-ray; In Dix-ie Land I'll take my stand, To live and die in Dix-ie, A-way, a-way, a-way down south in Dix-ie, A-way, a-way, a-way down south in Dix-ie.

Piano Chording

C F D₇ G₇

Chord letters appear throughout the song. These chords may be played on the autoharp. They may easily be played on the piano, too. Play the chords in the piano diagram over and over, until finding the right piano keys is easy. Then sing and play one chord a measure—as indicated.

Battle Hymn of the Republic

WORDS BY JULIA WARD HOWE
MUSIC BY WILLIAM STEFFE

1. Mine eyes have seen the glory of the coming of the Lord; He is trampling out the vintage where the grapes of wrath are stored; He hath loosed the fateful lightning of His terrible swift sword; His truth is marching on.

2. I have seen Him in the watch-fires of a hundred circling camps, They have builded Him an altar in the evening dews and damps; I can read His righteous sentence by the dim and flaring lamps; His day is marching on.

Refrain *Descant can be played or sung*

Glory, glory, glory, hallelujah!
Glory, glory, hallelujah!

134

During the War Between the States, Mrs. Howe visited an Army camp. Her return trip was slow—marching troops blocked the road. To pass the time, she and her companions sang songs—among them "John Brown's Body." This experience resulted in new, finer words for this old stirring tune.

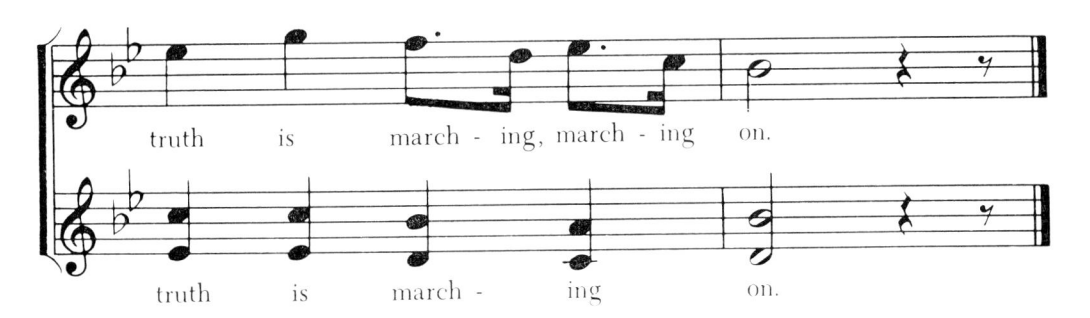

3. He has sounded forth the trumpet
   That shall never call retreat;
   He is sifting out the hearts of men
   Before the judgment seat.
   Oh, be swift, my soul, to answer Him!
   Be jubilant, my feet!
   Our God is marching on.

Tenting Tonight

WORDS AND MUSIC BY WALTER KITTREDGE

A popular camp song during the War Between the States.

1. We're tent-ing to-night on the old camp-ground,
   Give us a song to cheer Our wea-ry hearts, a song of home And friends we love so dear.

2. We've been tent-ing to-night on the old camp-ground,
   Think-ing of days gone by, Of the loved ones at home that gave us the hand, And the tear that said, "Good-bye."

Refrain

Man-y are the hearts that are wea-ry to-night, Wish-ing for the war to cease, Man-y are the hearts that are look-ing for the right, To see the dawn of peace. Tent-ing to-night, tent-ing to-night, Tent-ing on the old camp-ground.

136

3. We are tired of war
      on the old campground,
   Many are dead and gone,
   Of the brave and true
      who've left their homes,
   Others been wounded long.

4. We've been fighting today on the old campground,
   Many are lying near;
   Some are dead, and some are dying,
   Many are in tears.

Marines' Hymn

OFFICIAL SONG OF THE UNITED STATES MARINE CORPS

1. From the halls of Mon-te-zu-ma To the shores of Trip-o-li;____ We will fight our coun-try's bat-tles In the air, on land and sea;____ First to fight for right and free-dom And to keep our hon-or clean;____ We are proud to claim the ti-tle Of U-nit-ed States Ma-rine.____

2. Our____ flag un-furled to ev-'ry breeze From____ dawn to set-ting sun;____ We have fought in ev-'ry clime and place Where____ we could take a gun;____ In the snow of far-off north-ern lands And in sun-ny trop-ic scenes;____ You will find us al-ways on the job, The U-nit-ed States Ma-rines.____

3. Here's health to you and to our Corps
   Which we are proud to serve;
   In many a strife we've fought for life
   And never lost our nerve;
   If the Army and the Navy
   Ever look on Heaven's scenes,
   They will find the streets are guarded
   By United States Marines.

INSTRUMENTAL PARTS FOR THE SONG

Violin

B♭ Trumpets
B♭ Clarinets

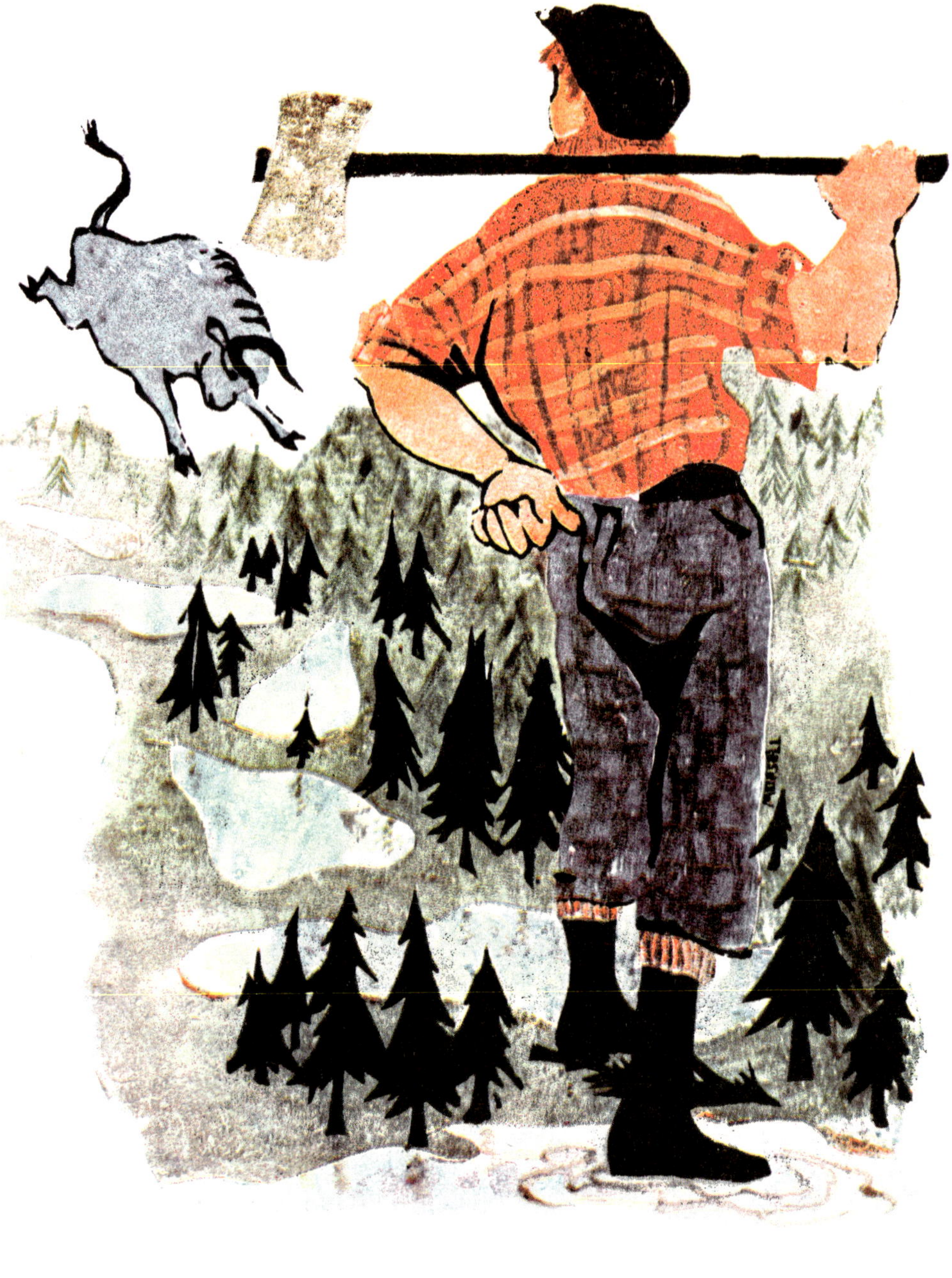

Paul Bunyan

WORDS BY RUTH MARTIN
MUSIC BY DYLAN TODD, ADAPTED

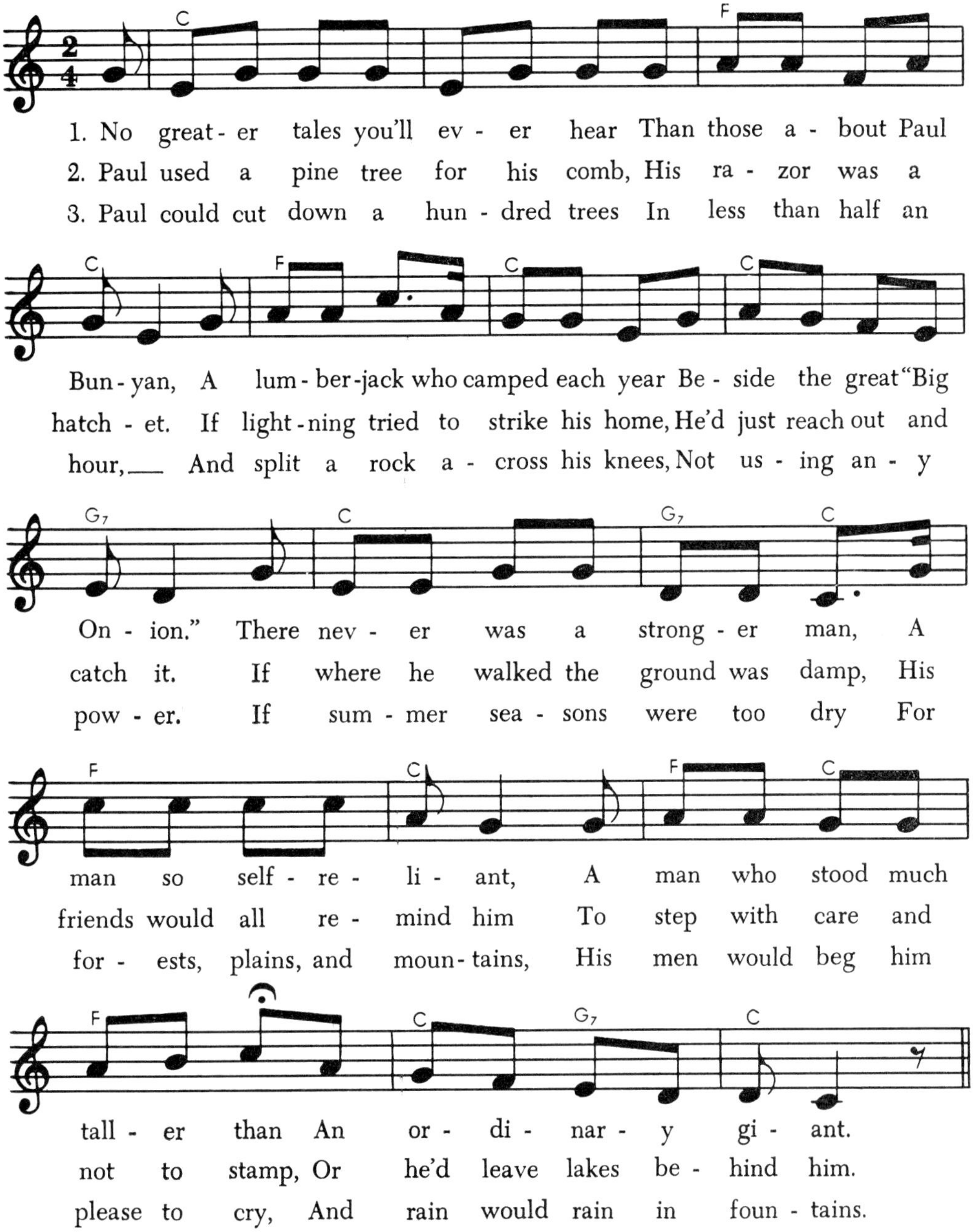

1. No great-er tales you'll ev-er hear Than those a-bout Paul Bun-yan, A lum-ber-jack who camped each year Be-side the great "Big On-ion." There nev-er was a strong-er man, A man so self-re-li-ant, A man who stood much tall-er than An or-di-nar-y gi-ant.

2. Paul used a pine tree for his comb, His ra-zor was a hatch-et. If light-ning tried to strike his home, He'd just reach out and catch it. If where he walked the ground was damp, His friends would all re-mind him To step with care and not to stamp, Or he'd leave lakes be-hind him.

3. Paul could cut down a hun-dred trees In less than half an hour, And split a rock a-cross his knees, Not us-ing an-y pow-er. If sum-mer sea-sons were too dry For for-ests, plains, and moun-tains, His men would beg him please to cry, And rain would rain in foun-tains.

141

Refrain

Paul Bun-yan! Paul Bun-yan! A might-y man was he!

    4. Paul never failed to aid a friend,
       No matter what the trouble.
       The helping hand that he would lend
       Would count for ten times double.
       There was no kind of work at all,
       No task he could not master.
       His friends were quick to call on Paul,
       But he would answer faster.

    5. If someone needed one strong breeze
       To launch a sailing schooner,
       He'd go to Paul and Paul would sneeze
       To launch the schooner sooner.
       If someone's dynamite gave out
       While blasting mountain passes,
       He'd go to Paul and Paul would shout,
       And mountains crashed in masses.

    6. Paul owned an ox who's famous too—
       A bright blue ox named Benny.
       If there were tricks he could not do,
       I've never heard of any.
       He'd haul two forests in one load
       And never seem to mind it,
       Or straighten out a crooked road,—
       He'd pull and just unwind it.

    7. Now Paul was good as he was tall,
       And kind as he was clever,
       But telling all the tales of Paul
       Would take me till forever.
       The more you grow, the more you'll hear
       About our friend Paul Bunyan,
       The lumberjack who camped each year
       Beside the great "Big Onion."

Joe Magarac

Slavic coal miners invented Joe Magarac and took him with them when they went to work in the steel mills. "Magarac" is the Slavish word for "fool." ... Joe was "a working fool."

WORK SONG OF THE STEEL MEN
BY JACOB A. EVANSON

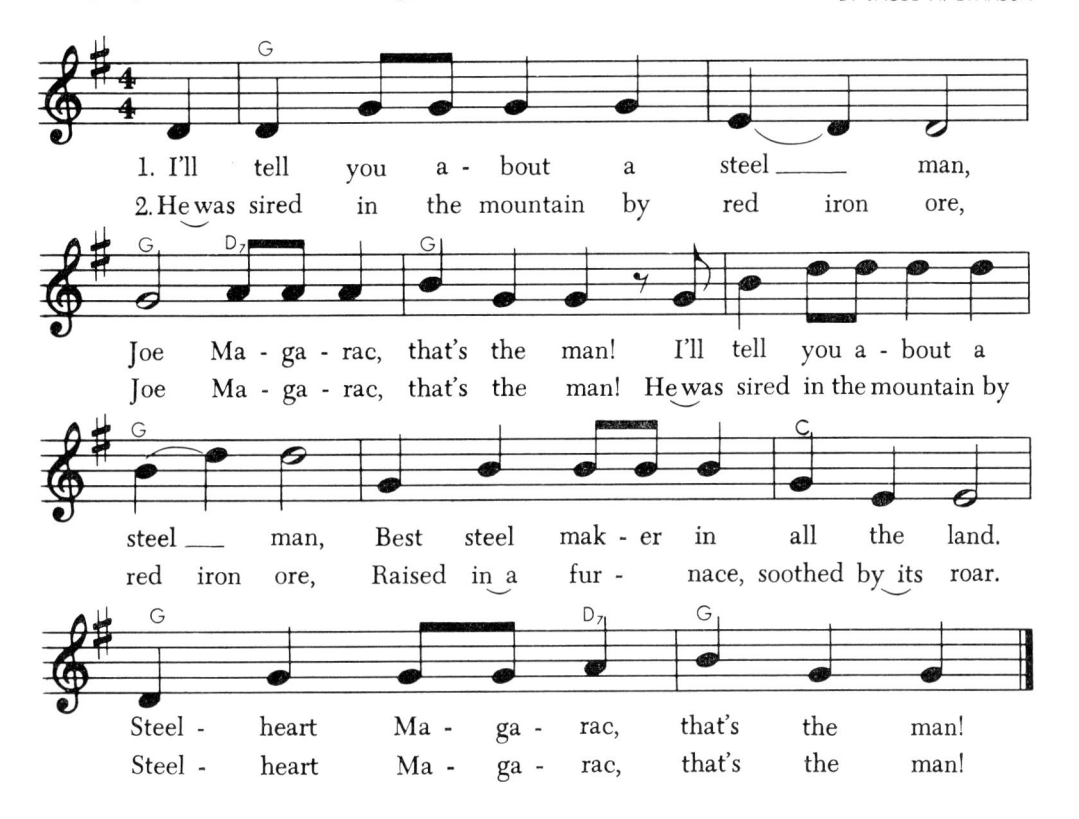

1. I'll tell you about a steel man,
   Joe Ma-ga-rac, that's the man!
   I'll tell you about a steel man,
   Best steel maker in all the land.
   Steel-heart Magarac, that's the man!

2. He was sired in the mountain by red iron ore,
   Joe Ma-ga-rac, that's the man!
   He was sired in the mountain by red iron ore,
   Raised in a furnace, soothed by its roar.
   Steel-heart Magarac, that's the man!

3. His shoulders are as big as the steel-mill door,
   Hands like buckets, his feet on half the floor.

4. With his hands he can load a half a ton dolly,
   He stirs the boiling steel with his fingers, by golly.

5. He grabs the cooling steel—his hands like wringers,
   And makes eight rails between his ten fingers.

6. Joe can walk on the furnace rim,
   From furnace to furnace—just a step for him.

7. Joe never sleeps, but he's got to eat,
   Hot steel soup, cold ingots for meat.

8. Now, if you think this man's not real,
   Then, jump in a furnace, see him cook the steel.

John Henry

WORK SONG FROM THE DEEP SOUTH

John Henry is a legendary hero whose fabulous prowess was celebrated by working men first in the South and later all over the country.

1. John Henry told his captain, "Well, a man ain't nothin' but a man, But before I let your steam drill beat me down, I'll die with a hammer in my hand. I'll die with a hammer in my hand."

2. Well, the captain says to John Henry, "Gonna bring that steam drill around, Gonna take that steam drill out on the job, Gonna whop that steel on down. Gonna whop that steel on down."

3. John Henry said to his shaker,
   "Shaker, why don't you sing?
   I'm throwin' twelve pounds from my hips on down,
   Just listen to that cold steel ring."

4. Well, the Captain says to John Henry,
   "I believe this mountain's cavin' in."
   John Henry said to the Captain,
   "'Tain't nothin' but my hammer suckin' wind."

5. They took John Henry to the buryin' ground,
   And they buried him in the sand;
   And every locomotive come roarin' round
   Says, "There lies a steel-drivin' man."

LANDS BEYOND THE STATES

Donkey Riding

The "donkey" these workers are riding is a donkey engine used for loading boats.

CANADIAN DOCK-LOADERS' SONG

1. Were you ev - er in Que - bec, Stow - ing tim - ber on the deck? Where there's a king with a gold - en crown, Rid - ing on a don - key.
2. Were you ev - er off the Horn, Where it's al - ways fine and warm? Seen the ___ lion and the un - i - corn, Rid - ing on a don - key.
3. Were you ev - er in Car - diff Bay, Where the folks all shout "Hoo - ray"? Here comes ___ John with his three months' pay, Rid - ing on a don - key.

Refrain
Hey, ho! A - way we go! Don - key rid - ing, don - key rid - ing,
Hey, ___ ho! A - way we go, Rid - ing on a don - key.

La Sandunga

WORDS BY MARGARET MARKS
MEXICAN FOLK SONG

The Tehuanas dance a simple waltz step to this typical Spanish melody with words addressed to Mother Earth.

1. The yel - low corn's ___ in the corn - field, ___
   The si - sal green ___ in the val - ley;
   The rush - es read - y for weav - ing, ___
   Thank you, our La - dy San - dun - ga.

2. The cat - tle graze ___ in the pas - ture, ___
   The lambs are heav - y with fleece now;
   The chick - ens plump ___ for the feast - ing, ___
   Thank you, our La - dy San - dun - ga.

Refrain

Ay, ___ San - dun - ga, ___ San - dun - ga, you ease our toil, Your prais - es we sing, San - dun - ga, ___ San - dun - ga, you bless our soil. ___

146

Pol Perica

Use drums and any kind of Latin American instruments you have to accompany this dance song.

TRANSLATED BY OLCUTT SANDERS
CHILEAN FOLK SONG

1. An-y-time Pe-ri-ca wish-es That her hus-band go to meet-ing, She a-ris-es Sun-day ear-ly, Irons his shirt with fan-cy pleat-ing.
2. An-y-time Pe-ri-ca wish-es That her hus-band eat his din-ner, She knows how he likes it par-boiled, Nei-ther of the two grows thin-ner.
3. An-y-time Pe-ri-ca wish-es That her hus-band show at-ten-tion, Then she doffs her dow-dy house-dress, Dons a blouse that mer-its men-tion.

Refrain
Oh, my Pe-ri-ca, hold your foot stead-y.
I'll tie your san-dals, Then you'll be read-y. read-y.

147

Shy Incognita

WORDS BY MARJORIE NEEFE
MUSIC ARRANGED BY E. JUREY

There is surprise and excitement on the last day of Mardi Gras when "Shy Incognita," the masked queen of the fiesta, removes her mask.

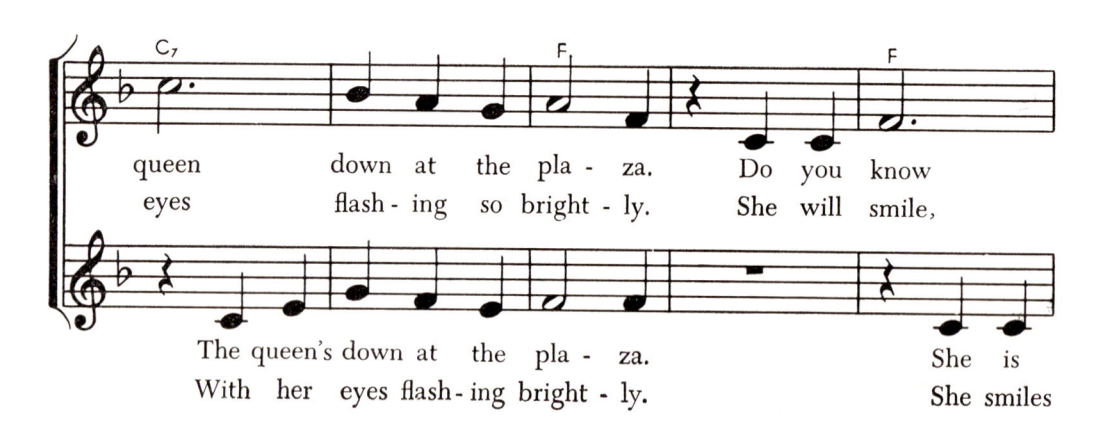

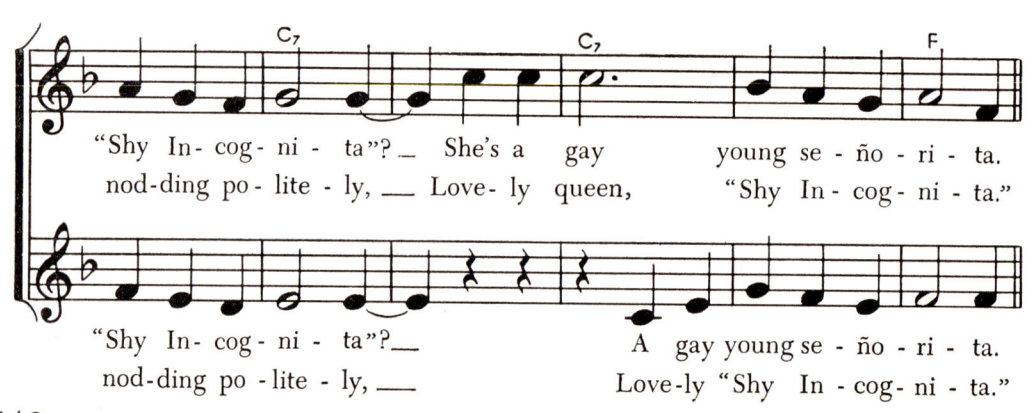

1. Let us go to the fi-es-ta!__ There's a queen down at the pla-za. Do you know "Shy In-cog-ni-ta"?__ She's a gay young se-ño-ri-ta.
2. She will dance whirl-ing so light-ly,__ With her eyes flash-ing so bright-ly. She will smile, nod-ding po-lite-ly,__ Love-ly queen, "Shy In-cog-ni-ta."

(harmony part)
We go to the fi-es-ta!__ The queen's down at the pla-za. She is "Shy In-cog-ni-ta"?__ A gay young se-ño-ri-ta.
She will dance, whirl-ing light-ly,__ With her eyes flash-ing bright-ly. She smiles nod-ding po-lite-ly,__ Love-ly "Shy In-cog-ni-ta."

Refrain

Hear the cas-ta-nets gai-ly play-ing,— while danc-ers—
are sway-ing.— Bright flow-ers be-fore her lay-ing,—
In hon-or of "Shy In-cog-ni-ta." our love-ly queen.—

Play throughout refrain

Castanets
Tambourines
Maracas

Jaqueta (Hah-kay-tah) is a short jacket.

Dance Song

WORDS BY MARGARET MARKS
CHILEAN FOLK SONG

1. To click-ing of cas-ta-net-a,— Jo-sé cir-cles round Jo-set-ta,— He's wear-ing a tight *ja-que-ta*— And moves with a cat-like grace.—
2. Jo-set-ta, her fin-gers snap-ping,— Turns slow-ly with heels a-tap-ping.— And now as they both start clap-ping,— They stamp and come face to face.—

Music from THE NEW AMERICAN SONG BOOK, Pan-American Edition, by Marx and Anne Oberndorfer, copyright 1933-1941 by Hall & McCreary Company. Used by permission.

Viva Panama

WORDS BY MARGARET MARKS
MUSIC COLLECTED BY AGNES DIXON

Long live Panama! This is what these Spanish words mean. Pronounced Kay-vee-va Pan-a-mah.

1. I came in-to town to sell my pig, The morn-ing aft-er Christ-mas; They gave me a spade and said to dig A ditch a-cross the Isth-mus.
2. I dug and I dug, the dirt just flew, The dig-ging was ter-rif-ic! I dug a can-al that joined the blue At-lan-tic and Pa-cif-ic.
3. And now, in the shade be-neath a tree, I watch each o-cean lin-er Go through the can-al from sea to sea, From sun-ny Spain to Chi-na.

Refrain: Qué vi-va, vi-va Pan-a-ma! Qué vi-va, vi-va Pan-a-ma! Qué vi-va, vi-va, vi-va,

150

vi - va Pan - a - ma! Qué vi - va, vi - va Pan - a - ma!

At the Gate of Heaven

Basques, brought from France, are today's sheep-herders in the West. These men do not mind this lonely life.

BASQUE FOLK SONG
COLLECTED IN NEW MEXICO

1. At the gate of heav'n they sell shoes for the an - gels,
2. God will send His bless - ing to all babes a - sleep - ing,

Lit - tle bare - foot an - gels, oh, come now and buy them.
God will help the moth - ers as watch they are keep - ing.

Refrain
Melody
Sleep, my baby, sleep, O my baby,
Sleep, my baby, a - rru, a - rru, my baby,

Sleep, O my baby, a - rru, a - rru.

Aloha Oe

HAWAIIAN SONG BY H. M. QUEEN LILIUOKALANI

*This is a poignant song of farewell.
Pronounce the title Ah-loh-hah Oy.*

Tune Ukulele
A D F♯ B

1. O'er the cliffs the rain-clouds proud-ly glide,
2. Mem-o-ries re-turn-ing from the past

As on-ward sweeps the gen-tle breeze;
Soon fill my sad and lone-ly bow'r,

How I long to have you at my side,
But you'll come to me a-gain, at last,

As the mist set-tles low through the trees.
And with long-ing I wait for that hour.

Refrain

Fare-well to thee, fare-well to thee, I
know that you'll come back to me some day;

Fare-well to thee, fare-well to thee,

152

Un - til we meet _____ a - gain. _____

*Meaning, "Farewell to Thee."

"Basay (bah-say) down"
means to sit down.

Basay Down

CALYPSO SONG FROM THE WEST INDIES

Ba - say, ma - ma, ba - say _____ down,

Fine

Oh, ba - say in the morn - in', ba - say _____ down.

Ba - say down, Miss Mar - y, ba - say _____ down, Ba - say

down, Miss Mar - y, ba - say _____ down; Ba - say down, Miss Mar - y,

D.C. al Fine

ba - say _____ down, Ba - say in the morn - in', ba - say _____ down.

Continue rhythms throughout

Drum R.H. / L.H.

Claves

Tambourine

Maracas

153

Calaloo

COLLECTED BY OLCUTT SANDERS
MUSIC FROM ST. CROIX, VIRGIN ISLANDS

Ev-'ry day is ca-la-loo. Ev-'ry day is ca-la-loo. All the beef and tur-keys, too. Noth-ing ev-er please me but this ca-la-loo. Set the ta-ble, let me eat while I'm a-ble, Crab and ca-la-loo. Tra la la la, tra la la la la, Tra la la la, tra la la la la, Tra la la la, tra la la la la. Crab and ca-la-loo.

Calaloo, a special stew made with many kinds of meat, is a favorite dish in the Virgin Islands. Rhythm is the thing in this song. Native singers beat it out on boxes or on anything at hand.

Bonita

WORDS BY MARGARET MARKS
PUERTO RICAN FOLK SONG

For introduction and throughout

1. Hey, Bo-ni-ta, hey, Hi, Bo-ni-ta, hi!
   Hey, Bo-ni-ta, hey, when you look my way I'm up in the sky. Your skin is as soft as satin, Your teeth are whiter than pearl, And there is no-bod-y sweet-er Than Bo-ni-ta, my best girl.

2. Hey, Bo-ni-ta, hey, Hi, Bo-ni-ta, hi!
   Hey, Bo-ni-ta, hey, there'll be ser-e-nades For you by and by. O beau-ti-ful se-ño-ri-ta, You put my heart in a whirl. She's on-ly sev-en months old now, But Bo-ni-ta's my best girl.

155

Sambalele

WORDS BY RUTH MARTIN
BRAZILIAN FOLK SONG

1. Hear how the mu-sic is play-ing, Dance to its light-heart-ed meas-ures, Clap-ping and stamp-ing and sway-ing, Join in the car-ni-val pleas-ures.
2. Dance while the drum-beat is pound-ing, Mel-low gui-tars soft-ly strum-ming, And cas-ta-nets clear-ly sound-ing, Join in the whis-tling and hum-ming.

Refrain:
Sam-ba, sam-ba, sam-ba-la-le-le, While we are danc-ing and sing-ing so gai-ly, Sam-ba, sam-ba, sam-ba-la-le-le, While we are danc-ing and sing-ing so gai-ly.

MANY PEOPLES—ONE NATION   *City Streets*

Only three thousand miles from east to west,
Only two thousand miles from north to south—
But all between
Where ten thousand points of light
Prick out cities, towns, villages.
　　　　　　　　—THOMAS WOLFE

We're All Together Again

BRITISH BOY SCOUT SONG

We're all to-geth-er a-gain, We're here, we're here.

We're all to-geth-er a-gain, We're here, we're here.

Who knows when we'll be all to-geth-er a-gain, Sing-ing

all to-geth-er a-gain? We're here, we're here!

157

Sidewalks of New York

WORDS BY CHARLES B. LAWLOR
MUSIC BY JAMES W. BLAKE

1. Down in front of Casey's___ Old brown wooden stoop,___ On a summer's evening___ We formed a merry group;___ Boys and girls together,___ We would sing___ and waltz,___ While an old man played the organ On the sidewalks of New York.___

2. Things have changed since those times,___ Some are up___ in "G,"___ Others, they___ are wand-'rers,___ But they all feel just like me,___ They'd part with all they've got,___ Could they but once___ more walk___ With___ their best girl and have a twirl On the sidewalks of New York.___

Refrain

East side, west side, all around the town,___ The tots sang "Ring-a-ro-sie," "London Bridge is fall - ing down." — Boys and girls to - geth - er, — Me and Ma - mie O' Rorke, — Tripped the light — fan - tas - tic On the side - walks of New York. —

Fashions

"Ole" (O-lay) means "Bravo!"
Pronounce "Tum" toom.

WORDS ADAPTED BY ELLEN WALES WALPOLE
BRAZILIAN POPULAR SONG ARRANGED BY HEITOR VILLA-LOBOS

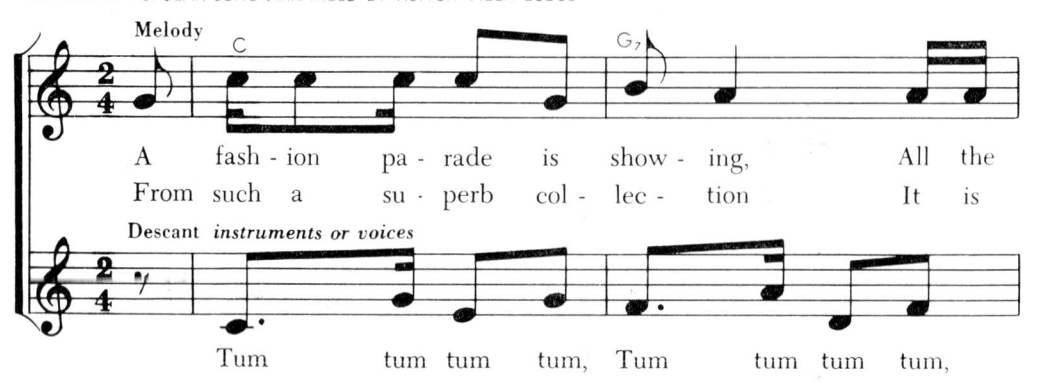

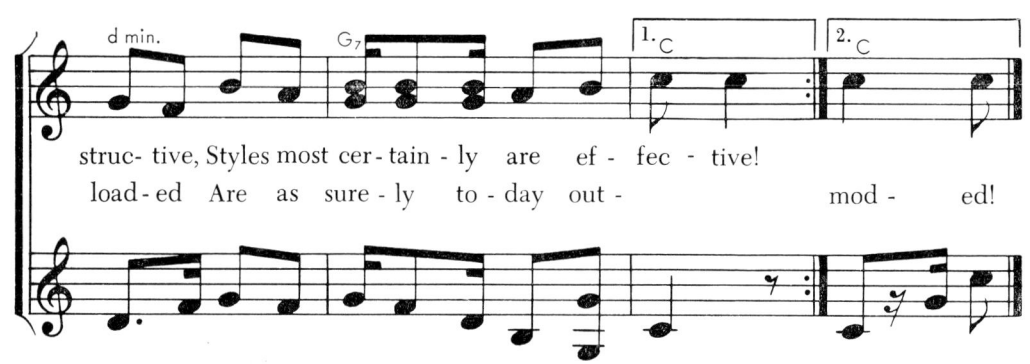

Melody:
A fash-ion pa-rade is show-ing, All the col-ors are bright and glow-ing, Though may-be not so con-struc-tive, Styles most cer-tain-ly are ef-fec-tive!

From such a su-perb col-lec-tion It is awk-ward to make se-lec-tion, For fash-ions with style once load-ed Are as sure-ly to-day out-mod-ed!

Descant (instruments or voices):
Tum tum tum tum, Tum tum tum tum, Tum tum tum tum, Tum tum tum tum, Tum tum tum tum, Tum tum tum tum, Tum tum tum tum tum, Tum! Tum! O-lé!

Street vendors sell different things in different cities.

Vendor's Song

WORDS BY LOUISE KESSLER
MEXICAN FOLK SONG

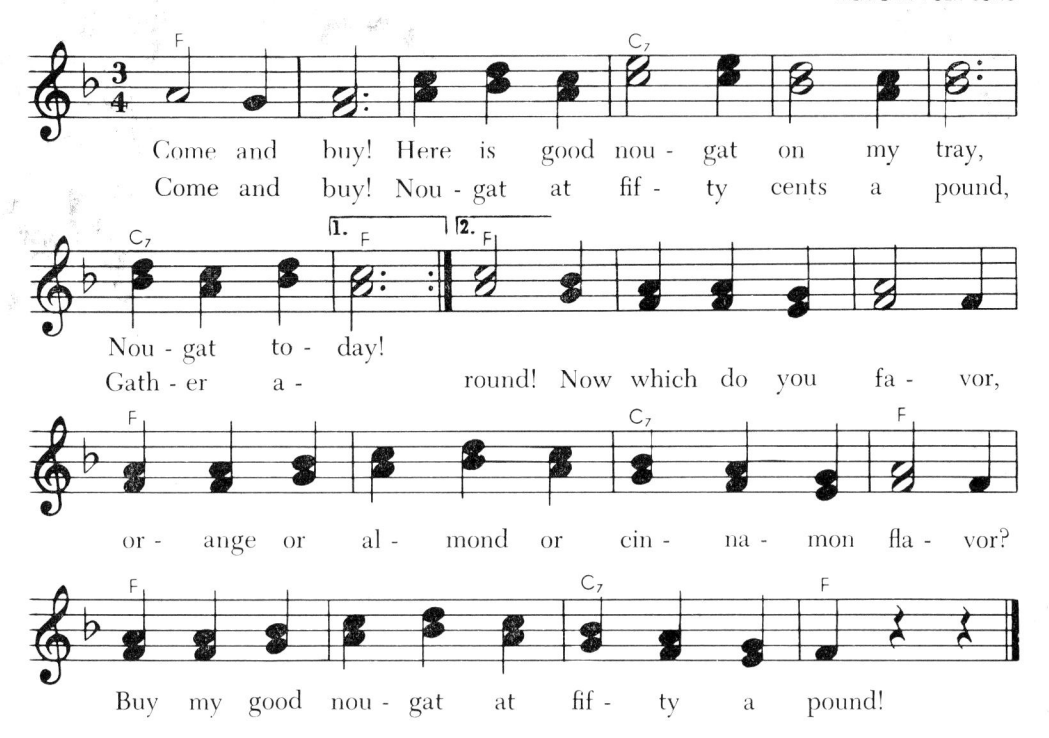

Come and buy! Here is good nou-gat on my tray, Nou-gat to-day!
Come and buy! Nou-gat at fif-ty cents a pound, Gath-er a-round! Now which do you fa-vor, or-ange or al-mond or cin-na-mon fla-vor? Buy my good nou-gat at fif-ty a pound!

On the Mall

EDWIN FRANKO GOLDMAN

Copyright 1923 by Carl Fischer, Inc., New York. Copyright renewed. Reprinted by permission.

Our Kites Are Flying

CHINESE FOLK SONG AS SUNG BY LI JENKUNG

1. Kites are flying overhead, Flying overhead,
   Floating in the air, Phantom wings outspread.
   Setting sun is glowing red, Glowing red.
   Blow, ye winds, and lift them to the sky;
   Kites are flying high, Kites are flying high, so high.

2. Mounting high and dipping low, Dipping swift and low,
   Sailing like a boat, Up and down they go.
   Gliding, sliding, to and fro, To and fro.
   Blow, ye winds, and lift them to the sky;
   Kites are flying high, Kites are flying high, so high.

Teru Teru Bozu

TRANSLATED BY ROBERT GARFIAS
JAPANESE FOLK SONG

Te - ru Te - ru bo - zu, Te - ru bo - zu,
To - mor - row bring us good weath - er all the day,
Like the sky I dreamt of___ On an eve - ning___ bright.
If you___ make the weath - er clear, I'll buy you___ gold - en bells.
Te - ru Te - ru bo - zu, Te - ru bo - zu,
To - mor - row bring us good weath - er all the day.

Teru Teru Bozu (Teh-roo Boh-zoo) is a small paper figure, gaily painted. It is a symbol of sunshine and is carried or hung under the eaves of houses with the hope that this will bring good weather.

Santa Lucia

NEAPOLITAN BOAT SONG

We can feel the pull of oars and also the gentle rocking waves in this Italian boat song.

1. Now 'neath the sil-ver moon O-cean is glow-ing,
2. When o'er thy wa-ters Light winds are play-ing,

O'er the calm bil-low Soft winds are blow-ing;
Thy spell can soothe us, All care al-lay-ing;

Here balm-y breez-es blow, Pure joys in-vite us,
To thee, sweet Na-po-li, What charms are giv-en,

And as we gent-ly row, All things de-light us.
Where smiles cre-a-tion, Toil blest by heav-en.

Refrain

Hark, how the sail-or's cry Joy-ous-ly ech-oes nigh:

San-ta Lu-ci-a! San-ta Lu-ci-a!

164

Home of fair po-e-sy, Realm of pure har-mon-y,

San-ta Lu-ci-a! San-ta Lu-ci-a!

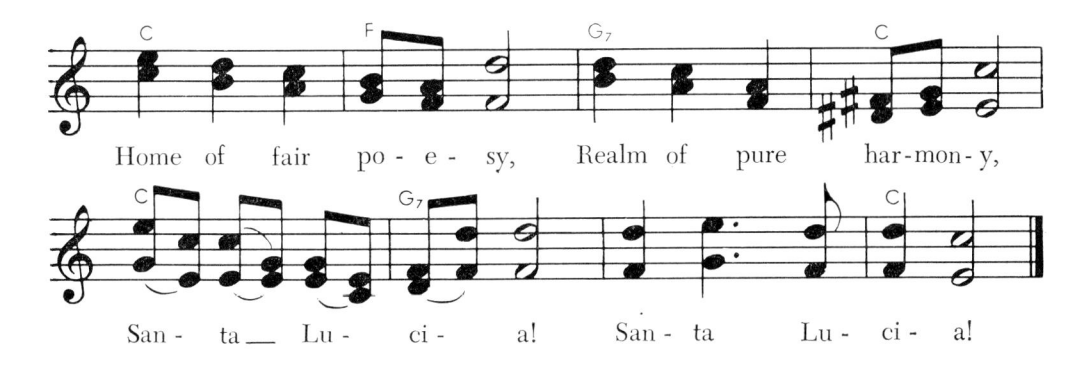

INSTRUMENTAL PARTS FOR THE SONG

Violins

B♭ Clarinets
B♭ Trumpets

Michie Banjo

WORDS BY MARGARET MARKS
LOUISIANA FOLK SONG ARRANGED BY CHARITY BAILEY

Our jazz comes from New Orleans street musicians, who often played on improvised instruments.

1. Look at Mich-ie Ban-jo, Fan-cy Mich-ie Ban-jo, Strut-tin' down the street. Cha-peau cocked on one side, Mich-ie Ban-jo, High but-ton shoes that squeak, Walk-in' stick a-swing-in' wide, Mich-ie Ban-jo, Ev-'ry-thing's all com-plete.

2. Look at Mich-ie Ban-jo, Fan-cy Mich-ie Ban-jo, Strut-tin' down the street. Di-mon' pin in his tie, Mich-ie Ban-jo, Bright yal-ler gloves so neat. Trous-ers pleat-ed way up high, Mich-ie Ban-jo, Ev-'ry-thing's all com-plete.

Refrain

Look at Mich-ie Ban-jo, Fan-cy Mich-ie Ban-jo, Strut-tin' down the street. Does-n't he look sweet, Strut-tin' down the street!

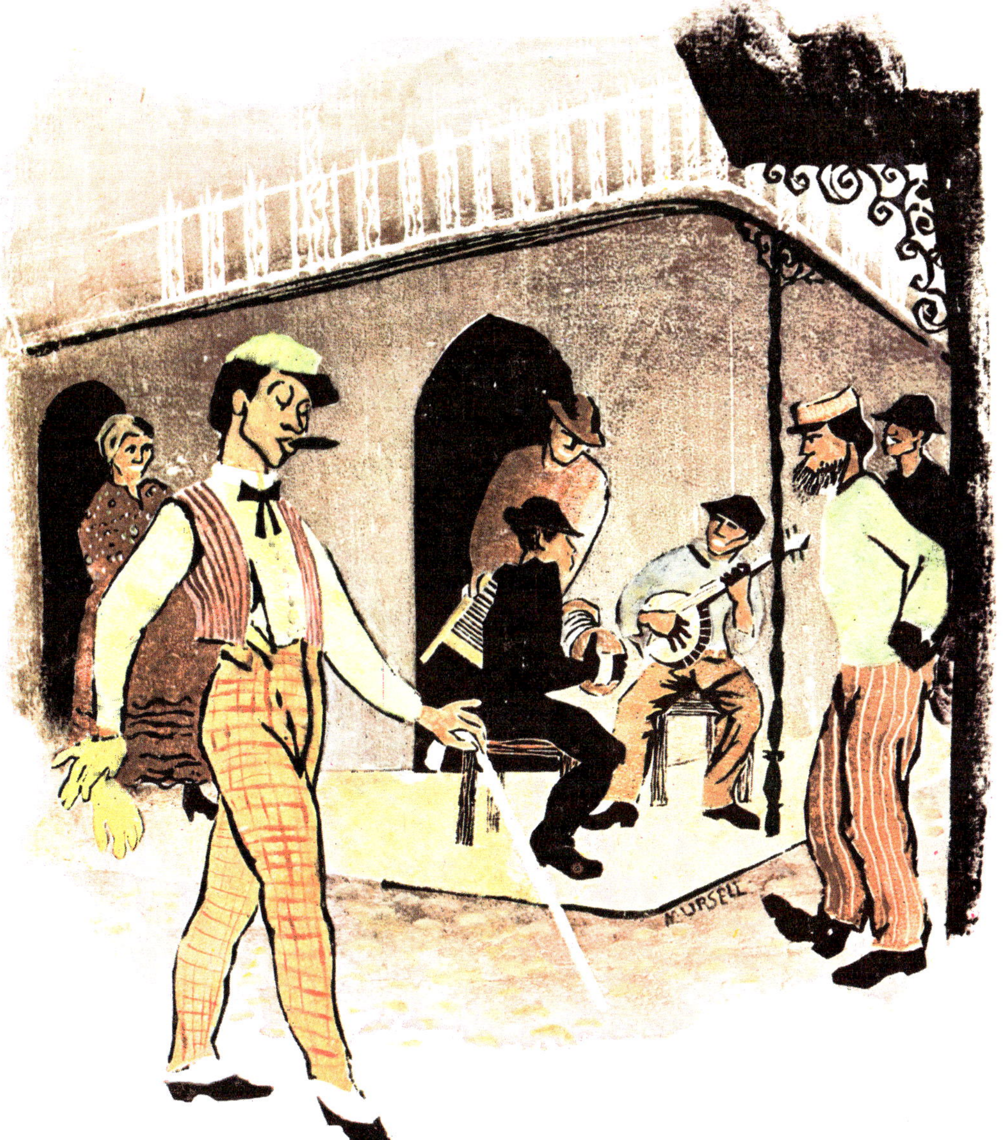
M. URSELL

Bells

WORDS BY VIVIAN COOPER
FRENCH ROUND

*There are many bells in a big city,
which clang together to tell
people what time of day it is.*

Church bells at noon go ding dong ding, Church bells at noon go cling clang cling.

Hear them as they ring through the sun-shine of morn-ing, Hear them as they sing o-ver

streets of the town. Ring-ing, sing-ing bells that go ding ding dong.

Brahms' Lullaby

WORDS FROM THE GERMAN
MUSIC BY JOHANNES BRAHMS

*Play chords on piano
or individual tone bars (resonator bells)*

1. Lull-a-by and good-night, With roses be-dight,
2. Lull-a-by and good-night, Thy moth-er's de-light,

With lil-ies o'er-spread is ba-by's wee bed;
Bright an-gels be-side my dar-ling a-bide;

168

Lay thee down now and rest, may thy slum-ber be blest;
They will guard thee at rest, thou shalt wake on my breast;

Lay thee down now and rest, may thy slum-ber be blest.
They will guard thee at rest, thou shalt wake on my breast.

Zum Gali Gali

PALESTINIAN FOLK SONG

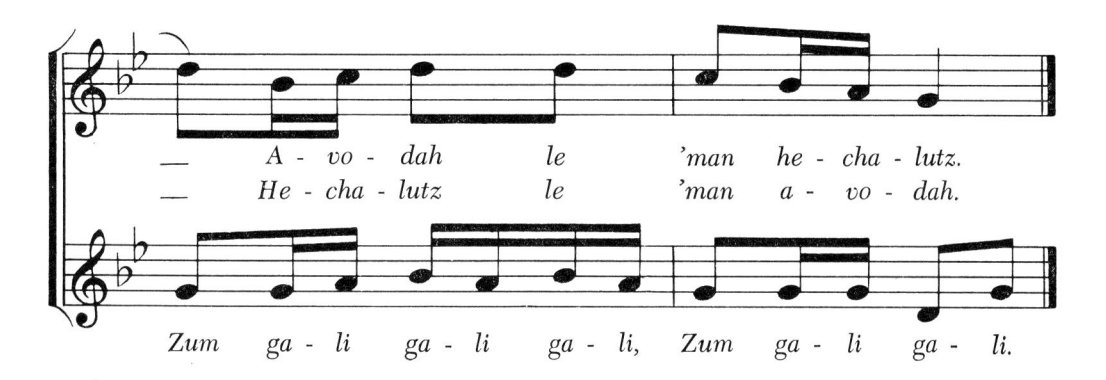

1. He - cha - lutz le 'man a - vo - dah;
2. A - vo - dah le 'man he - cha - lutz;

Zum ga - li ga - li ga - li, Zum ga - li, ga - li,

A - vo - dah le 'man he - cha - lutz.
He - cha - lutz le 'man a - vo - dah.

Zum ga - li ga - li ga - li, Zum ga - li ga - li.

The Hebrew words of this song mean that the pioneer's purpose is labor. Pronounce *"Zum ga-li,"* zoom gah-lee; *"He-cha-lutz le 'man a-vo-dah,"* Hay-kah-lootz le mahn ah-voh-dah.

The Sponge Diver

WORDS BY MARGARET MARKS
GREEK MELODY COLLECTED BY MARGARET MARKS

Many Greeks have come from the Old World to dive for sponges in the warm waters off Florida.

1. From Kalymnos* sailed a fishing boat Out, out to sea, Out, out to sea. Sailed away to waters where the sponges grow, Sailed away to dive for them way down below, Sailed away, and all the women watched them go Out to the sea, the everlasting ocean, Out, out to sea.

2. Then the divers from the fishing boats Dove down in the sea, Dove down in the sea. Dove for sponges all along the ocean floor, Diving dives of fifty yards and maybe more, Diving deeper than they ever dove before Down in the sea, the everlasting ocean, Down, down in the sea.

*An island off the coast of Greece

3. Back to harbor sailed the fishing boat,
   Home, home from the sea; home, home from the sea.
   Home with sponges strung along atop the mast,
   Home again, the terrors of the sea are past,
   Home again, the weary men are safe at last.
   Home from the sea, the everlasting ocean,
   Home, safely, from the sea.

Las Mañanitas

ENGLISH WORDS BY CAROL RAVEN
MEXICAN FOLK SONG

Dar - ling, wake! The shad - ows fly, The sleep - y moon has said good bye, Come and greet the rose of dawn - ing, And say good morn - ing to me.

On the streets the lights are out, Lamp - light - er knows what he's a - bout, Knows that day will o - pen eyes, And bring sun - ny skies, too, no doubt.

I'll step out of doors at dawn - ing, I'll climb up a mag - ic stair, And bring down the stars of morn - ing To make a crown for your hair.

Deitch Company

GERMAN FOLK SONG

Drum— *introduction and throughout*

Oh, when you hear the roll of the big bass drum,
Then you may know that the Deitch have come; For the
Deitch Com - pa - ny is the best com - pa - ny, That
ev - er came o - ver from old Ger - ma - ny.

Refrain
Ho - ra, ho - ra, ho - ra la la la la, Ho - ra, ho - ra,
ho - ra la la la la, Tra la la la la,____
Tra la la la la,____ Heis mine oys - ter raw.

Shusti-Fidli

CZECHOSLOVAKIAN FOLK SONG

Add a new instrument each time, after singing the verse. Then add all the instruments previously sung about, in reverse order. "Play" them, as you sing.

Verse
"Can you guess what I have here?" "Tell us, tell us, John-ny dear." "A fid-dle to make mu-sic gay." "Come and show us how you play."

Refrain Fiddle
1. Shus-ti fid-li fid-li, Shus-ti fid-li fid-li, Here's how (the/it) fid-dle plays, plays.

Clarinet
2. Diu-dli-diu-dli-em, Diu-dli-diu-dli-em, Here's how (the/it) clari-net plays, plays.

Trumpet
3. Tra-da-da, Tra-da-da, Here's how (the/it) trum-pet plays, plays.

Bass Viol
4. Brmm-fitz-fitz, Brmm-fitz-fitz, Here's how (the/it) bass viol plays, plays.

Drums
5. Boom! Ching! Drrr! Boom! Ching! Drrr! Here's how (the/they) drums all play, play.

Orchestra
6. (whistle) Here's how (the/they) or-ches-tra plays, play.

173

Country Lanes

In singing this old song, substitute the name of the city nearest to you.

I Found a Horseshoe

RAILROAD SONG FROM ILLINOIS AND IOWA

I found a horse-shoe, I found a horse-shoe. I picked it up and nailed it on the door; And it was rust-y and full of nail holes, Good luck 'twill bring to you for-ev-er-more.

Verse

1. The man who owned the horse, he lived in New York,
2. The horse that wore the shoe, his name was Mike,

The man who owned the horse, he lived in New York.
The horse that wore the shoe, his name was Mike.

The man who owned the horse, The man who owned the horse, The
The horse that wore the shoe, The horse that wore the shoe, The

D.C. al Fine

man who owned the horse, he lived in New York.
horse that wore the shoe, his name was Mike.

175

Down in the Valley

KENTUCKY FOLK SONG

A well-loved song around which Kurt Weill has woven his folk opera of the same title.

1. Down in the valley, the valley so low,
   Hear the winds blow, dear, hear the winds blow,
   Hang your head over, hear the winds blow.

2. Writing this letter, containing three lines,
   Will you be mine, dear, will you be mine?
   Answer my question, will you be mine?

3. Build me a castle forty feet high,
   So's I can see him as he goes by.
   As he goes by, dear,
   As he goes by,
   So's I can see him as he goes by.

From THE SINGIN' GATHERIN' by Jean Thomas, the "Traipsin' Woman," and Joseph A. Leeder, published by Silver Burdett Company. Reprinted by permission.

The Happy Plowman

In singing the refrain, use "he" the first time and "she" the second time.

TRANSLATED BY MRS. ALBERT MAGNUSON
SWEDISH FOLK SONG

1. Near a home in a wood, With a horse ver-y good,
A poor young farm-er smiled as he stood
Look-ing down at his plow; In his heart was a glow,
Then he sang as he plowed the row:

2. In the house near the wood, where the farm-er stood,
There lived his help-mate, love-ly and good;
As she cooked and she stirred, She was glad that she heard,
And she ech-oed ev-'ry word:

Refrain
"Heigh-ho, my lit-tle but-ter-cup! We'll dance un-til the sun comes up!" Thus {he/she} sang as {he plowed,/she stirred,} And {he/she} smiled as {he/she} sang, While the woods and the wel-kin rang.

177

Woodman, Spare That Tree

WORDS BY GEORGE P. MORRIS
MUSIC BY HENRY RUSSELL

Swinging gently in their lawn swings, people in the Victorian era sang this song with great emotion.

1. Wood-man, spare that tree! Touch not a sin-gle bough; In youth it shel-tered me, And I'll pro-tect it now; 'Twas my fore-fa-ther's hand That placed it near his cot; There, wood-man, let it stand, Thy axe shall harm it not.

2. When but an i-dle boy, I sought its grate-ful shade; In all their gush-ing joy, Here, too, my sis-ters played. My moth-er kissed me here; My fa-ther pressed my hand; For-give this fool-ish tear, But let that old oak stand.

3. That old fa-mil-iar tree, Whose glo-ry and re-nown Are spread o'er land and sea, And wouldst thou hack it down? Woodman, for-bear thy stroke! Cut not its earth-bound ties; Oh, spare that a-ged oak, Now tow-'ring to the skies!

4. My heartstrings round thee cling, Close as thy bark, old friend! Here shall the wild bird sing, And still thy branch-es bend. Old tree! The storm still brave! And, wood-man, leave the spot: While I've a hand to save, Thy axe shall harm it not.

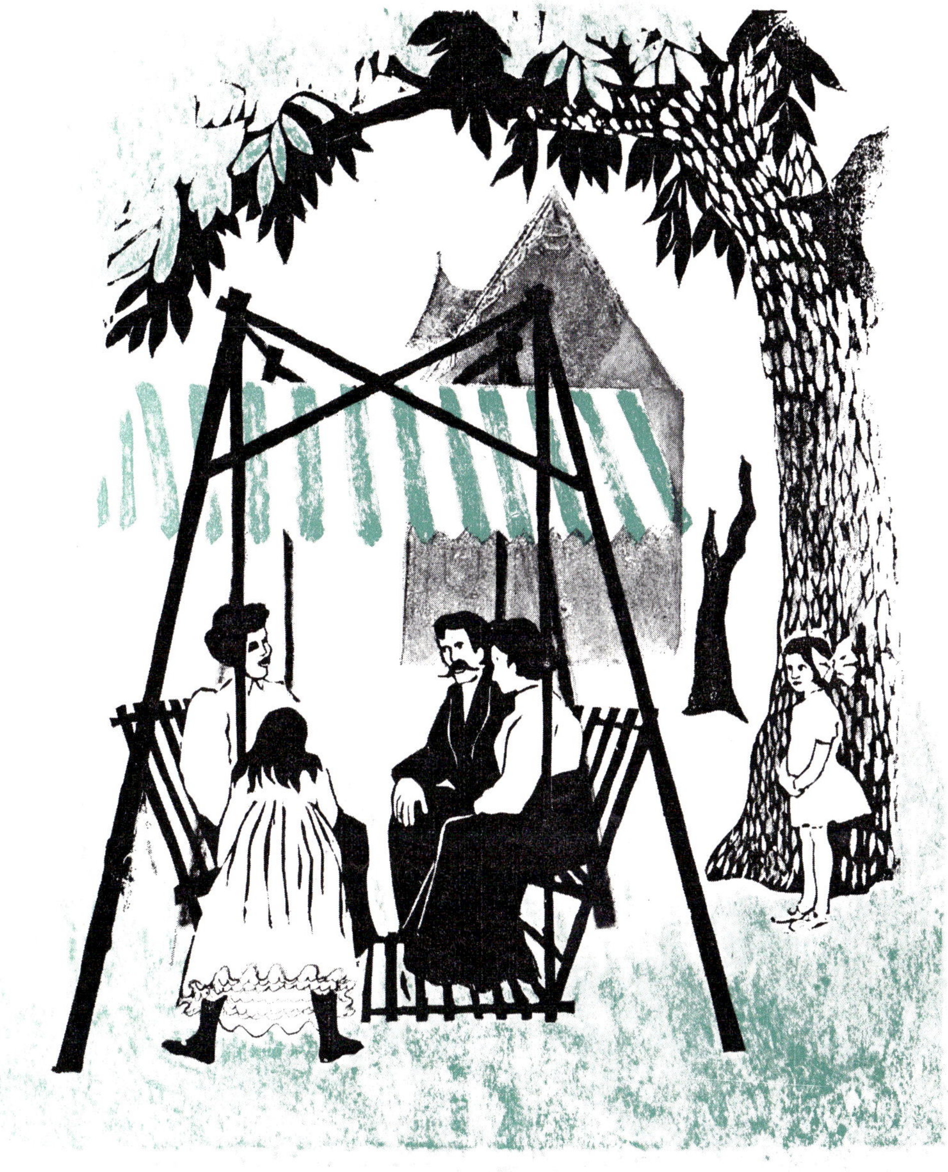

Stodola Pumpa

WORDS ADAPTED
CZECHOSLOVAKIAN FOLK SONG

"Stodola pumpa" means barn pump.
Pronounce it stow-dah-lah pum-pah, with
the "u" in "pum" like "oo" in book.

1. Walk-ing at night, with laugh and mer-ry song,
   'Neath rus-tling trees we slow-ly walk a-long.
   Walk-ing at night, with laugh and mer-ry song,
   'Neath rus-tling trees we slow-ly walk a-long.___ Hey!

2. Birds twit-t'ring soft-ly at the close of day,
   Stars glim-m'ring through to light our home-ward way.
   Birds twit-t'ring soft-ly at the close of day,
   Stars glim-m'ring through to light our home-ward way.___

Refrain

Sto-do-la sto-do-la sto-do-la pum-pa,
Sto-do-la pum-pa, sto-do-la pum-pa, pum, pum, pum.

The Farmer

This flowing melody from Cuba describes the movement of the river and the busy farmer, both.

ENGLISH WORDS ADAPTED
MUSIC BY ZOILA ROSA LOPEZ FUNDORA

Near where the riv-er is flow-ing
stands a white house in the coun-try.
There lives a farm-er who works to
keep his crops all green and grow-ing,
Plow-ing and till-ing the soil from ear-ly
morn till set of sun, Talk-ing and sing-ing and
feast-ing when the work of day is done.

181

Under the Shady Trees

FOLK SONG FROM CENTRAL LUZON, THE PHILIPPINES
COLLECTED BY PETRONA RAMOS

Ear-ly in the dawn-ing, Gai-ly we were go-ing
Through the sun-ny morn-ing, Where ripe fruit was grow-ing.
We saw *man-gos* yel-low, Red *ma-co-pas* rare,
With a kind-ly fel-low Bid-ding us wel-come there.
"En-ter, friends, eat your fill.
Here are fruits de-li-cious. Here are *si-ni-gue-las* sweet.
Mel-ons ripe are now a treat.

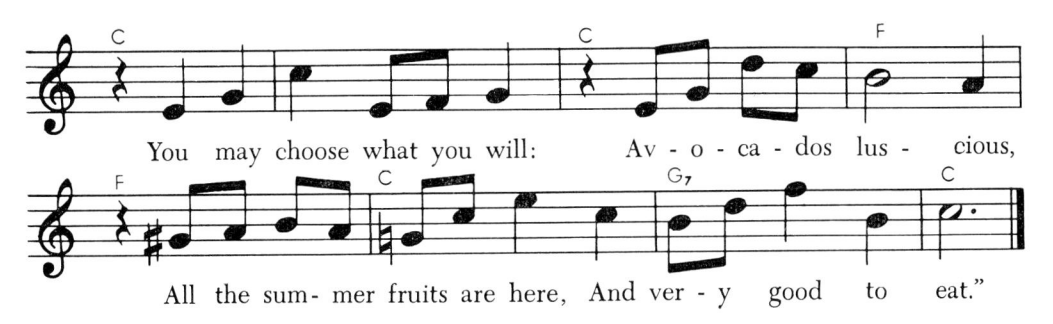

"You may choose what you will: Avocados luscious,
All the summer fruits are here, And very good to eat."

Mangos (mahn-gohss) are imported to America. *Macopas* (mah-coh-pahss) look like small red apples; they grow on cone-shaped trees. *Siniguelas* (seen-ee-gay-lahss) are small, yellow, and round.

Sing Everyone

WORDS ADAPTED
GERMAN ROUND

I. Sing a tune, ev'ry-one, sing on your way.
II. Sing forth a happy song, sing when the world seems wrong,
III. Melody warms the heart, lightens the day.

Himmel und Erde müssen vergehn, Aber die Musici, aber die Musici, Musici bleiben bestehn.

(Himmel oont Ehrduh muessen fehrgayn, Ahbehr dee Moosikee, Ahbehr dee Moosikee, Moosikee blighben beshtayn.)

183

Bones

FOLK SONG FROM SOUTHERN UNITED STATES

Limber up your wrist bone and clap a rhythmic accompaniment.

Oh, the bones, oh, the bones, oh, the jee-ump-in' bones,
Oh, the bones, oh, the bones, oh, the jee-ump-in' bones,
Oh, the bones, oh, the bones, oh, the jee-ump-in' bones,
Oh, ___ did-n't it rain!

1. Oh, the toe bone con-nect-ed to the foot bone, And the foot bone con-nect-ed to the an-kle bone, And the an-kle bone con-nect-ed to the leg bone, Oh, ___ did-n't it rain!

2. Oh, the leg bone con-nect-ed to the knee bone, And the knee bone con-nect-ed to the thigh ___ bone, And the thigh ___ bone con-nect-ed to the hip bone, Oh, ___ did-n't it rain!

3. Oh, the hip bone connected to the back bone,
   And the back bone connected to the neck bone,
   And the neck bone connected to the head bone.

4. Oh, the finger bone connected to the hand bone,
   And the hand bone connected to the elbow bone,
   And the elbow bone connected to the shoulder bone.

5. Oh, the shoulder bone connected to the back bone,
   And the back bone connected to the neck bone,
   And the neck bone connected to the head bone.

Walking Song

Capture the effect of this yodel echoing across Alpine valleys. Sing Hol-dee-ree-ah.

WORDS BY MARTHA DABNEY
SWISS FOLK TUNE

1. Up the hill and down the way, Hol-di-ri-di-a hol-di-ri-a,
   We shall wear no shoes to-day, Hol-di-ri-di-a hol-di-a.
2. No more shoes than fish-es wear, Hol-di-ri-di-a hol-di-ri-a,
   In the brook that wan-ders near, Hol-di-ri-di-a hol-di-a.
3. Bare-foot as the birds we'll roam, Hol-di-ri-di-a hol-di-ri-a,
   Up the hills and down, and home, Hol-di-ri-di-a hol-di-a.

Refrain
Hol-di-ri-di-a hol-di-ri-di-a, hol-di-ri-a,
Hol-di-ri-di-a, hol-di-ri-di-a hol-di-a.

So Long

WORDS AND MUSIC BY WOODY GUTHRIE

1. I've sung this song but I'll sing it a-gain,
Of the place where I lived on the wild wind-y plains,
In the month called A-pril, the coun-ty called Gray,
And here's what all of the peo-ple there say:

2. A dust storm hit and it hit like thunder,
It dust-ed us o-ver and cov-ered us under,
It blocked out the traf-fic and blocked out the sun,
And straight for home all the peo-ple did run, sing-ing:

Refrain

"So long, it's been good to know you, So long, it's been good to know you, So long, it's been good to know you, This dust-y old dust is a-get-ting my home, I've got to be mov-ing a-long."

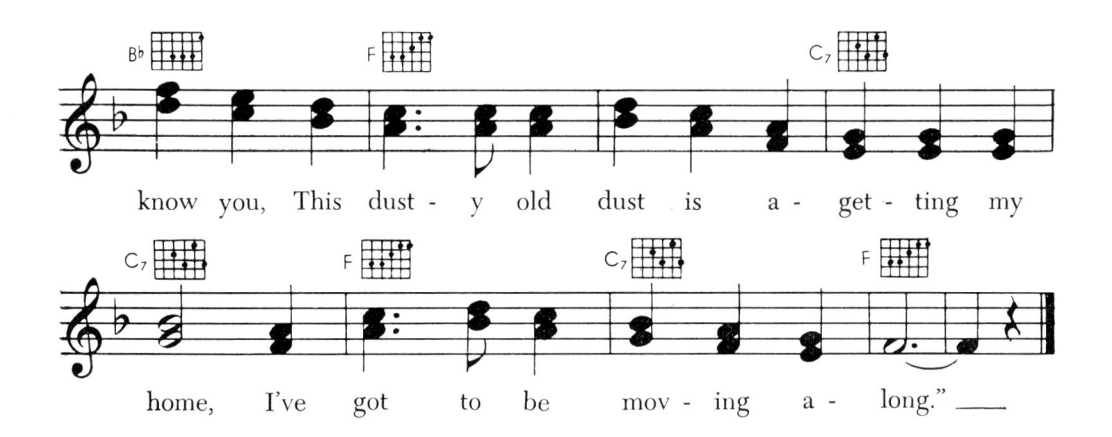

3. We talked of the end of the world, and then
   We'd sing a song, and then sing it again.
   We'd set for an hour and not say a word,
   And then these words would be heard:

Copyright 1954 by Folkways Music Publishers, Inc.,
New York, N.Y. International copyright secured.
All rights reserved. Used by permission.

Hunting Song

ENGLISH FOLK SONG

I. Mer - ri - ly, mer - ri - ly greet the morn,
II. Cheer - i - ly, cheer - i - ly sound the horn,
III. Hark to the ech - oes, hear them play, O'er
IV. hill and dale and far a - way.

187

Fiesta

Festivals and Dances

PARAPHRASED BY MARY BUDLONG
FOLK SONG FROM MEXICO

(All) 1,3. A light gui-tar in the dusk soft-ly strum-ming,
(Boys) 2. Now with a sweet se-ño-ri-ta I'm danc-ing,

From near and far now the danc-ers are com-ing.
A red, red rose in her hair, how en-tranc-ing!

The gold-en lan-terns a-bove us are swing-ing,
And in her heart, as we're glid-ing and sway-ing,

And on the soft eve-ning air voi-ces ring, tra la la la!
I fond-ly hope sweet Chi-qui-ta will say, tra la la la!

Refrain

(Boys) 1,3. We'll do a lit-tle dance to-geth-er,
(Girls) 2. We'll do a lit-tle dance to-geth-er,

Chi-qui-ta is the one for me!
Pe-ri-co is the one for me!

We'll do a lit-tle dance to-geth-er,

188

D. C. al Fine

Chi - qui - ta is the one for me!
Pe - ri - co is the one for me!

Play throughout refrain

Tambs
Castanets
Claves

Feasting by the Ocean

*Poi (poy) is taro root, pounded and fermented.

WORDS BY WILLIAM HUGHES
HAWAIIAN MELODY

1. Comes the day of feast-ing and danc-ing,
2. All a-bus-tle, ev-'ry-bod-y work-ing,
3. Ho! the wood-en bowls up-on the ta-ble,

Comes the morn-ing clear and en-chant-ing,
Call-ing, laugh-ing, ev-'ry-bod-y stir-ring,
Each to hold as much as it is a-ble,

Comes the fish-er shout-ing of his catch-ing,
Pig a-cook-ing, ten-der for the eat-ing,
Five a per-son, man-y more for serv-ing,

Bus-y since the peep of ear-ly morn-ing.
Poi* up-on the ta-ble set for man-y.
Read-y for the feast-ing by the o-cean.

From THE NEW AMERICAN SONG BOOK, Pan-American Edition, copyright 1933-41 by Hall & McCreary Company. Used by permission.

Tostadas

ENGLISH WORDS BY JULIA W. BINGHAM
MUSIC BY MIGUEL ANGEL COBOS

Tortillas that are fried crisp and served with chili and cheese are "tostadas" (tohs-tah-dahss.)

Come, buy tos-ta-das, they're such a treat!
Tos-ta-das brown sim-ply can't be beat.
So crack-ling crisp, bak-ing on the grid-dle,
With chil-i too, they're so good to eat.
Then add some cheese, melt-ed yel-low gold,
With cof-fee strong, have it hot or cold.
At one for five, bet-ter two for ten,
Just try them once, you'll come back a-gain!

Navajo Happy Song

NAVAJO INDIAN SONG

Hi yo, hi yo ip si ni yah, hi yo, Hi yo ip si ni __ yah, hi __ yo, Hi yo ip si ni yah,

(Last time only)

hi __ yo, Hi yo ip si ni yah, Ip si ni yah!

Widdicombe Fair

ENGLISH FOLK SONG

1. Tom Pearse, Tom Pearse, lend me your gray mare,
2. And when shall I see a-gain my gray mare?
3. Then Fri-day came, and Sat-ur-day noon,

All a-long, down a-long, out a-long lee,
All a-long, down a-long, out a-long lee,
All a-long, down a-long, out a-long lee,

For I want for to go to Wid-di-combe Fair,
By Fri-day soon, or Sat-ur-day noon,
But Tom Pearse-'s old mare has not trot-ted home,

Refrain

Wi' Bill Brew-er, Jan Strew-er, Pe-ter Gur-ney,

Pe-ter Da-vy, Dan'l Whid-don, Har-ry Hawk,

Old Un-cle Tom Cob-leigh, and all,

Old Un-cle Tom Cob-leigh, and all.

4. So Tom Pearse he got up to the top o' the hill,
   All along, down along, out along lee,
   And he seed his old mare down a-making her will,

5. So Tom Pearse's old mare, her took sick and died,
   All along, down along, out along lee,
   And Tom he sat down on a stone and he cried,

6. When the wind whistles cold on the moor of a night,
   All along, down along, out along lee,
   Tom Pearse's old mare doth appear ghastly white,

7. And all the long night he heard skirling and groans,
   All along, down along, out along lee,
   From Tom Pearse's old mare in her rattling bones,

Rodeo Time

GROUP OF CHILDREN
HUNTINGTON BEACH ELEMENTARY SCHOOL, CALIFORNIA

Through clouds of dust, Hoofs beat-ing the ground,
With twirl-ing ri-a-tas, Va-que-ros ride on.
Down in the can-yons, Ear-ly at dawn,
Round-ing up cat-tle, The ro-de-o is on!

At rodeo time (roh-day-oh) the cattle are rounded up so that an owner can find out how many he has. "Riata" (ree-ah-tah) comes from the Spanish and means "lariat." "Vaqueros" (vah-kay-rohss) are "cowboys."

Mexican Hat Dance

WORDS BY LISBETH RAWSKI
MEXICAN DANCE

Spanish gentlemen toss their sombreros before the dancing senorita. She dances around the brim of one—thus choosing her partner.

Oh, would you like to trav-el to Je-rez?
To see the mar-kets at the fi-es-ta,
Pa-pa-yas, man-gos, and en-chi-la-das,
Ta-ma-les, hot chi-le, and tos-ta-das,
Come to the mar-ket on fi-es-ta day.
Bright se-ra-pes, high som-bre-ros, Sil-ver belts and jin-gling

Papayas (pah-pah-yas) and *mangos* (mahn-gohs) are fruits. *Enchiladas* (Ehn-tchee-lah-dahss) and *tamales* (tah-mah-layss) are delicacies made of meat and cornmeal. *Chile is* pronounced chee-leh. Fiesta-goers wear bright shawls—*serapes* (seh-rah-payss), wide brimmed *sombreros* (sohm-bray-rohss), and sandals—*huaraches* (hoo-rah-tchayss).

ear-rings, Straw *hua-ra-ches* light for danc-ing, Made for danc-ing on wide hat brims. At the pla-za at the fies-ta.

Interlude

Fast-er, fast-er, yet a lit-tle fast-er, Fast-er, fast-er, gai-ly spin a-long.

With the mu-sic shake your knee, With the mu-sic shake your toe.

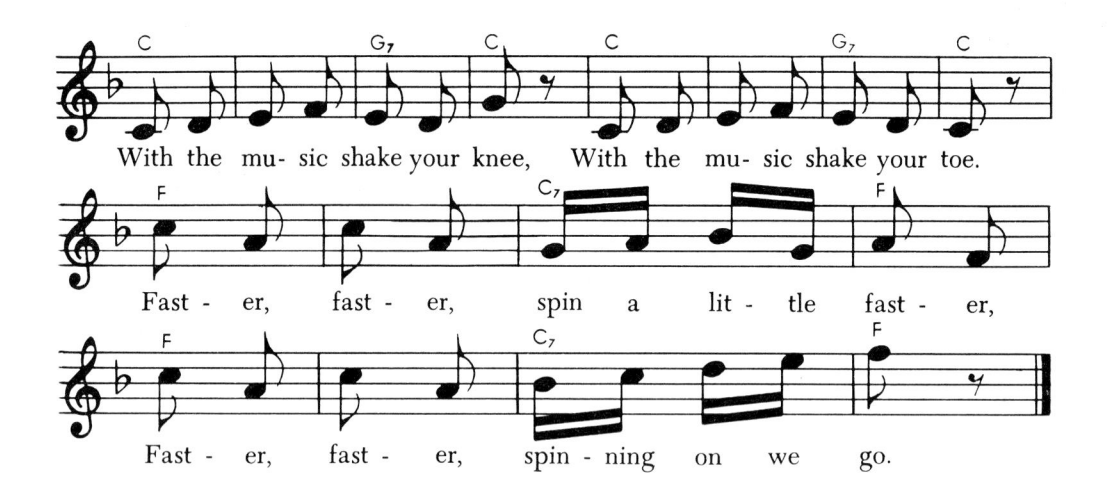

With the mu-sic shake your knee, With the mu-sic shake your toe.
Fast-er, fast-er, spin a lit-tle fast-er,
Fast-er, fast-er, spin-ning on we go.

The Beautiful Blue Danube

WORDS BY FREDERICK H. MARTENS
MUSIC BY JOHANN STRAUSS

So clear and blue,

Melody

Beau-ti-ful stream,_____ A ra-di-ant

We sing to you; The

dream,_____ The sky seems to flow,_____

stream so bright, Re - flects the
With you as you're go - - - -

light. And gay the song
ing. And gay is the song You

You bear a - long, Shores that you
car - ry a - long, By shores that you lave,

lave, Lave with your wave; A - way to join the sea!
With your wave, On your way to join the sea!

Song of the Gypsy King

WORDS BY ALICE WHITE
TRADITIONAL CZECHOSLOVAKIAN DANCE

1. Gyp - sies all, it's here we'll be stay - ing,
   The dark - ness falls, no time for de - lay - ing!
   These woods our home, this grass for our bed, And
   our roof those branch - es high o - ver head.

2. Faith - ful po - nies here we will teth - er,
   Then build our fire, eat sup - per to - geth - er.
   We'll pop a fat hen in - to the pot, It
   makes no big dif - f'rence where Hon - za got it!

Refrain
Fire - light wink - ing, Star - light twin - kling,
'Neath the moon We dance and we sing.

3. Polka round me stamping and clapping,
   Now this way, that way, tambourines rapping,
   We whirl and twirl as campfires gleam bright,
   For a polka is the gypsies' delight.

The melody of this song is a traditional folk dance.

INSTRUMENTAL PARTS FOR THE SONG

Song of Destiny

WORDS ADAPTED
TRADITIONAL HEBREW MELODY

1. Look toward the east, whence comes the glowing light,
Golden horizon, heralding the day.
Faith beckons you with promise ever bright.
Hope will abide with you along the way.

2. Lift your heart, break forth in joyous song,
Sing for the blue sky's promise of the day.
Friends who are true, and friends who are strong,
Join in our song to help us on our way.

Refrain
Climb on upward, dauntless soul!
Onward, steadfast, toward the distant goal!
Steadfast, courageous, hope will lead you on your quest.
There in the east, the mountain's golden crest!

200

ROUND THE CALENDAR

*Autumn was kind to them,
Winter was long to them—
But in April, late April,
All the gold sang.*
—THOMAS WOLFE

Rain Music

WORDS BY JOSEPH COTTER, JR.
MUSIC BY MILTON KAYE

1. On the dust-y earth-drum, Beats the fall-ing rain;
2. Chords of earth a-wak-ened, Notes of green-ing spring,

Now a whis-per-ing mur-mur, Now a loud-er strain.
Rise and fall___ tri-um-phant O-ver ev-'ry-thing.

Refrain
Slen-der sil-ver-y drum-sticks, On the an-cient drum,
Beat the mel-low mu-sic, Bid-ding life to come. A-wake!

The Seasons

WORDS BY NANCY BYRD TURNER
MUSIC BY JEAN SIBELIUS

At the close of the first growing season, Pilgrims in New England praised God for their crops—the first Thanksgiving Day.

1. The sea - sons come, the sea - sons go, And God has planned them all. He makes the win - ter wind to blow, The au - tumn leaves to fall; And when the balm - y spring - time De - scends on wood and hill, His word goes forth, the leaves re - turn, And grass and bud and daf - fo - dil.

2. The weath - er is the plan of God; He sends the frost and snow, The pleas - ant rain up - on the sod Where wheat and bar - ley grow. And then the long year fol - lows Like an - swer to His call, And ev - 'ry time is bless - ing time, For God has wise - ly planned them all!

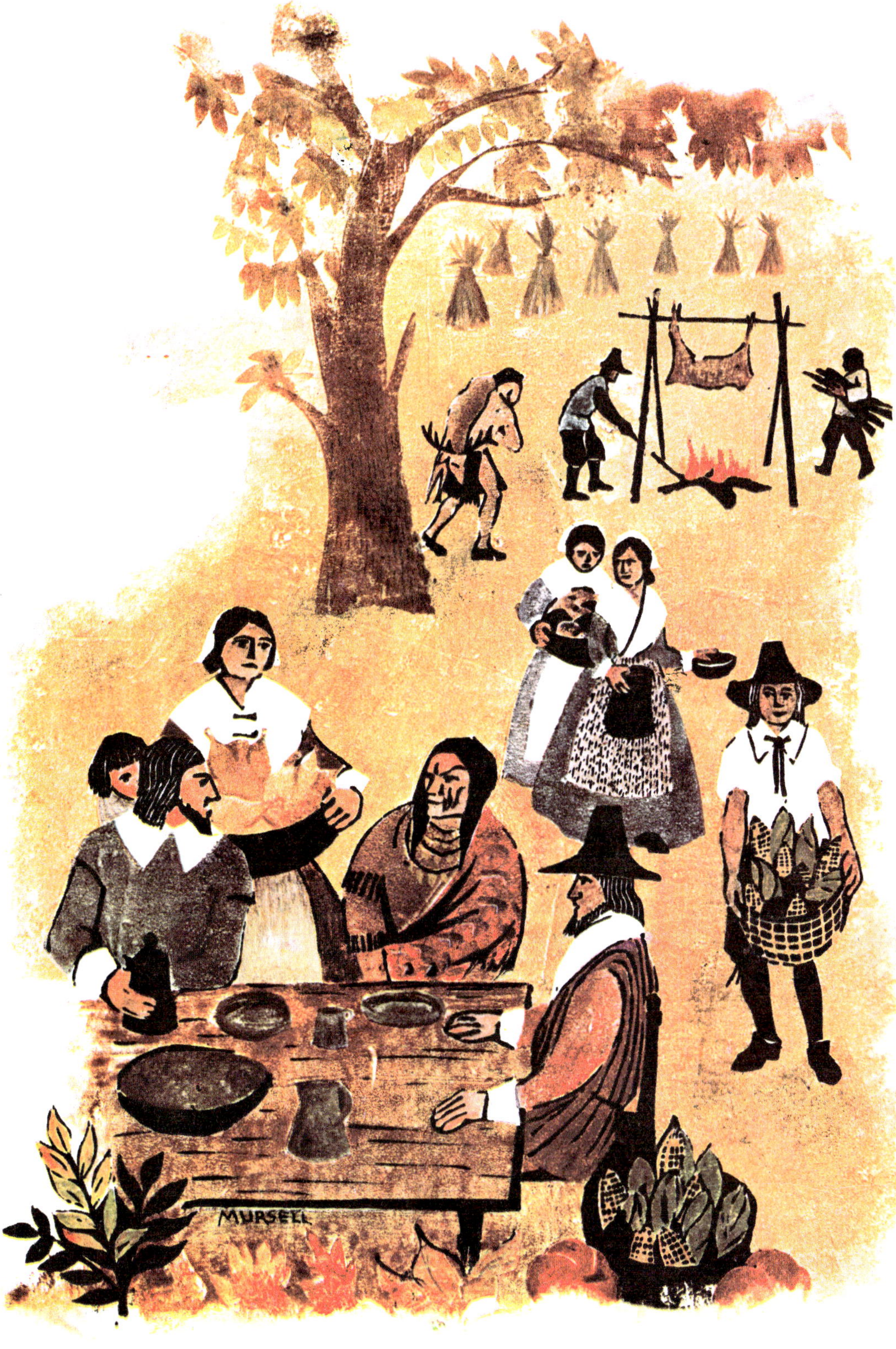
MURSELL

Harvest Hymn

WORDS BY HENRY ALFORD
MUSIC BY GEORGE J. ELVEY

1. Come, ye thank-ful peo-ple, come, Raise the song of har-vest home; All is safe-ly gath-ered in, Ere the win-ter storms be-gin; God, our Mak-er, doth pro-vide For our wants to be sup-plied; Come to God's own tem-ple, come, Raise the song of har-vest home.

2. All the bless-ings of the field, All the stores the gar-den yield; All the fruits in full sup-ply, Rip-ened 'neath the sum-mer sky; All that spring with boun-teous hand Scat-ters o'er the smil-ing land; All that lib-'ral au-tumn pours, From her rich o'er-flow-ing stores.

3. These to Thee, our God, we owe, Source from which all bless-ings flow; And for these our souls shall raise Grate-ful vows and sol-emn praise; Come, then, thank-ful peo-ple, come, Raise the song of har-vest home; Come to God's own tem-ple, come, Raise the song of har-vest home.

Whatsoever things are true,
Whatsoever things are honest,
Whatsoever things are just,
Whatsoever things are pure,
Whatsoever things are lovely,
Whatsoever things are of good report;
If there be any virtue,
And if there be any praise,
I will think on these things.
—PHILIPPIANS 4:8

Now Thank We All Our God

ENGLISH WORDS BY CATHERINE WINKWORTH
MUSIC ARRANGED BY JOHANN CRUGER

Now thank we all our God, With hearts and hands and voi-ces, Who won-drous things hath done, In whom His world re-joi-ces; Who, from our moth-ers' arms, Hath blessed us on our way, With count-less gifts of love, And still is ours to-day.

Sleigh Ride

WORDS BY FREDERICK H MARTENS
UKRAINIAN FOLK SONG

Bells are needed to simulate the sound of the sleigh bell on this dashing sleigh.

1. Pound-ing hoof and flow-ing mane, Bit-ing airs that tin - gle,
2. On, you po-nies, hep, hep, hep! There is naught to bind you.

Out a-cross the snow-y plain The sil - ver sleigh-bells jin - gle,
On the steppe, be-neath the stars, Now leave the wind be-hind you!

206

Out a-cross the snow-y plain The sil-ver sleigh-bells jin - gle!
On the steppe, be-neath the stars, Now leave the wind be-hind you!

Lonely Is the Hogan

TRANSLATED BY DERRICK N. LEHMER
NAVAJO INDIAN SONG

When snow falls cold and deep on the flat-topped foothills of the southwestern mountains, the Navajos retire to their hogans—earth-covered lodges.

1. Lone-ly is the ho-gan, ___ The birds are still.
   No more ___ the wild flow-ers bloom on the hill.
2. White up-on the me-sa ___ The win-ter snow,
   Cold blows ___ the wind through ___ the can-yon be-low.

Christmas Lullaby

WORDS BY RUTH MARTIN
TRADITIONAL MEXICAN CAROL

In a low-ly man-ger the shep-herds have found Thee,____ All the shin-ing glo-ry of heav-en a-round Thee.____

Refrain

There, on high, the great star is beam-ing, Dear__ Child, slum-ber sweet-ly dream-ing.____

The Shepherds

ADAPTED BY VIRGINIA HARRISON
FOLK CAROL FROM POLAND

1. Sheep on the hill-side, sheep on the hill-side, Sleep-ing in the shad-ow, Si-lence a-round them, si-lence a-round them, Fold-ing field and mead-ow. Si-lent, the shep-herds
2. Stars up a-bove them, stars up a-bove them, Mov-ing on-ward slow-ly, One star a-mong them, one star a-mong them, Gleam-ing high and ho-ly. Look, how it seems to

watch there be - side them, Si - lent, the shep - herds
lead through the dark - ness, Look, how it seems to

watch there be - side them, While their watch they're keep - ing,
lead through the dark - ness, Guid - ing safe - ly, sure - ly,

All the world is sleep - ing, Nev - er night so still as this night!
Shin - ing clear - ly, pure - ly, Nev - er light so fair as this light!

Christmas Is Coming

WORDS AND MUSIC BY F. NESBITT

1. Christ - mas is com - ing! The goose is get - ting fat!
2. If you've no pen - ny, A ha' - pen - ny will do,

Please to put a pen - ny in an old man's hat,
If you have no ha' - pen - ny, Then God bless you,

Please to put a pen - ny in an old man's hat.
If you have no ha' - pen - ny, Then God bless you.

From GIRL GUIDE SONGS. Reprinted by permission of Novello and Company, Ltd.

We Three Kings

WORDS AND MUSIC BY JOHN HENRY HOPKINS

1. We three kings of O - ri - ent are,
   Bear - ing gifts we trav - erse a - far,
   Field and foun - tain, moor and moun - tain,
   Fol - low - ing yon - der star.

2. Born a Babe on Beth - le - hem's plain,
   Gold we bring to crown Him a - gain;
   King for ev - er, ceas - ing nev - er,
   O - ver us all to reign.

Refrain

O — star of won - der, star of might,
Star with roy - al beau - ty bright,
West - ward lead - ing, still pro - ceed - ing,
Guide us to thy per - fect light.

3. Frankincense to offer have I;
   Incense owns a Deity nigh,
   Prayer and praising all men raising,
   Worship Him, God on high.

4. Myrrh is mine; its bitter perfume
   Breathes a life of gath'ring gloom;
   Sorrowing, sighing, bleeding, dying,
   Sealed in the stone-cold tomb.

Silent Night

WORDS BY JOSEPH MOHR
MUSIC BY FRANZ GRUBER

1. Si - lent night, ho - ly night, All is calm, all is bright Round yon Vir - gin Moth - er and Child, Ho - ly In - fant so ten - der and mild, Sleep in heav - en - ly peace, Sleep in heav - en - ly peace.

2. Si - lent night, ho - ly night, Shep - herds quake at the sight, Glo - ries stream from heav - en a - far, Heav - 'nly hosts sing, "Al - le - lu - ia; Christ, the Sav - iour is born! Christ, the Sav - iour is born!"

Hark! the Herald Angels Sing

WORDS BY CHARLES WESLEY
MUSIC BY FELIX MENDELSSOHN

1. Hark! the herald angels sing, "Glory to the new-born King;
Peace on earth, and mercy mild,— God and sinners reconciled!"
Joyful all ye nations, rise,— Join the triumph of the skies;—
With the angelic host proclaim, "Christ is born in Bethlehem."

Refrain
Hark! the herald angels sing, "Glory to the new-born King."

2. Christ, by highest heav'n adored,— Christ, the everlasting Lord;
Late in time behold Him come,— Offspring of the Virgin's womb.
Veiled in flesh the God-head see;— Hail the Incarnate Deity,—
Pleased as man with man to dwell, Jesus our Emmanuel!

3. Mild He lays His glory by,
Born that man no more may die,
Born to raise the sons of earth,
Born to give them second birth.
Ris'n with healing in His wings,
Light and life to all He brings,
Hail the Sun of Righteousness!
Hail, the heav'n-born Prince of Peace!

INSTRUMENTAL PARTS FOR THE SONG

Purim Song

WORDS BY JUDITH EISENSTEIN
JEWISH FOLK SONG

1. Who's that mak-ing all the noise? Who are those pa-rad-ers?
2. Pu-rim rat-tle leads the line In his strip-ed jack-et;
3. Ha-man and the jol-ly King Mor-de-cai and Es-ther,

They are on-ly girls and boys, Pu-rim mas-quer-ad-ers.
Pop-py seed cakes, Ha-man hats, Don't they make a rack-et!
Wind-ing up the big pa-rade Comes the Pu-rim jes-ter.

La la la la la la la, La la la la la la,

La la la la la la la. Pu-rim mas-quer-ad-ers.

White Coral Bells

TWO-PART ROUND

I
1. White cor-al bells up-on a slen-der stalk,
2. Oh, don't you wish that you could hear them ring?

II
Lil-ies of the val-ley deck my gar-den walk.
That will hap-pen on-ly when the fair-ies sing.

New Created World

FROM THE ORATORIO "THE CREATION"
FRANZ JOSEPH HAYDN

A new cre-a-ted world, a new cre-a-ted world Springs up, springs up at God's com-mand. A new cre-a-ted world, a new cre-a-ted world Springs up, springs up at God's com-mand, Springs up at God's com-mand, springs up at God's com-mand.

Shepherd's Dance

INCIDENTAL MUSIC TO "HENRY VIII"
EDWARD GERMAN

Reprinted by permission of the copyright owner, Novello & Co., Ltd.

May

WORDS BY RUTH MARTIN
MUSIC BY WOLFGANG AMADEUS MOZART

1. We welcome you, sweet May-time,
The time of wonderful spring, And days of care-free
play-time When larks and nightingales sing;
The time when meadows and trees are green,
And fragrant violets grow, When skies above are
blue and serene, And whispering breezes blow.

2. In May the sun is glowing,
So warm and gentle and gold, The brooks and streams are
flowing, The lambs are peaceful in fold.
With happy laughter the whole day long
We merrily go on our way, Through fields and woodland
singing a song In welcome to wonderful May.

216

MORE SONGS TO SING

The year's at the spring
And day's at the morn;
Morning's at seven;
The hillside's dew-pearled;
The lark's on the wing;
The snail's on the thorn;
God's in his heaven—
All's right with the world!
—ROBERT BROWNING

Home

WORDS ANONYMOUS
GERMAN FOLK SONG

1. Home, home, can I for-get thee? Dear, dear, dear-ly loved home.
2. Home, home, why did I leave thee? Dear, dear friends, do not mourn.

No, no, still I re-gret thee, Though I may far from thee roam.
Home, home, once more re-ceive me, Quick-ly to thee I'll re-turn.

Refrain

Home, home, home, home, Dear-est and hap-pi-est home.

Jeanie with the Light Brown Hair

WORDS AND MUSIC BY STEPHEN FOSTER

I dream of Jean-ie with the light brown hair, Borne, like a va-por, on the sum-mer air; I see her trip-ping where the bright streams play, Hap-py as the dai-sies that dance on her way. Man-y were the wild notes her mer-ry voice would pour, Man-y were the blithe birds that war-bled them o'er; Oh! I dream of Jean-ie with the light brown hair, Float-ing, like a va-por, on the soft, sum-mer air.

The American Hymn

WORDS AND MUSIC
BY MATTHIAS KELLER

1. Speed our Re-pub-lic, O Fa-ther on high, Lead us in path-ways of jus-tice and right! Rul-ers as well as the ruled, one and all, Gir-dle with vir-tue, the ar-mor of might! Hail! three times hail to our coun-try and flag! Rul-ers as well as the ruled, one and all, Gir-dle with vir-tue, the ar-mor of might! Hail! three times hail to our coun-try and flag!

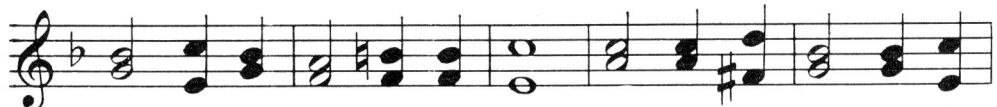

2. Rise up, proud ea-gle, rise up to the clouds! Spread thy broad wings o'er this fair west-ern world! Fling from thy beak our dear ban-ner of old! Show that it still is for free-dom un-furled! Hail! three times hail to our coun-try and flag! Fling from thy beak our dear ban-ner of old! Show that it still is for free-dom un-furled! Hail! three times hail to our coun-try and flag!

Symphonic Themes

When listening to recordings of these symphonies, or when attending a concert at which they are performed, try to recognize the well-known themes printed below and identify the instruments that play them.

Symphony No. 94, in G Major, "Surprise"
FRANZ JOSEF HAYDN, 1732-1809

2nd Movement - *Andante*

Symphony No. 40, in G Minor
WOLFGANG AMADEUS MOZART, 1756-1791

1st Movement - *Allegro molto*

Symphony No. 3, in E-flat Major, "Eroica"
LUDWIG VAN BEETHOVEN, 1770-1827

1st Movement - *Allegro con brio*

Symphony No. 8, in B Minor, "Unfinished"
FRANZ SCHUBERT, 1797-1828

1st Movement - *Allegro moderato*

Symphony No. 1, in C Minor
JOHANNES BRAHMS, 1833-1897

4th Movement - *Allegro non troppo, ma con brio*

Finlandia

WORDS BY FREDERICK H. MARTENS
MUSIC BY JEAN SIBELIUS

O land of lakes and az - ure streams a - flow-ing,___
Whose woods of larch and pine are green al - way,___
Where can - did skies and wa - ters blue a - glow-ing___
Come from a - bove their tri - bute to pay,___
And na - ture's God is beau - ty rare be - stow ing;___
May it en - dure, Fin - land - ia, for aye!___

This melody is a part of the symphonic poem *Finlandia*. As with so much of Sibelius' music, it has the quality of a folk melody and has attained the status of an unofficial Finnish national anthem.

A Song About a Day

WORDS BY JANE ROLFE RANDOLPH
CZECH FOLK SONG

1. Sun - light, sun - light, shin - ing on ev - 'ry home;
2. Twi - light, twi - light, shad - ows are long and deep;

Sun - light, sun - light, morn - ing has come.
Twi - light, twi - light, soon we shall sleep.

We'll find this gold - en day Hap - py with work and play;
Each hour that rolled a - way Made this a hap - py day;

Sun - light, sun - light, morn - ing has come!
Twi - light, twi - light, soon we shall sleep.

A Pledge

WORDS BY MARGARET MANN
MUSIC BY WOLFGANG AMADEUS MOZART

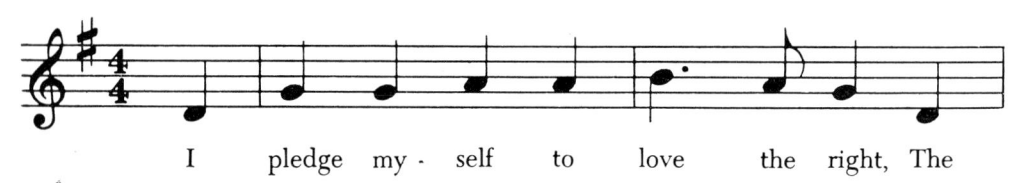

I pledge my - self to love the right, The

good, the fair and true, To keep my faith and hon-or bright In ev-'ry-thing I do.

Come, Thou Almighty King

WORDS BY CHARLES WESLEY
MUSIC BY FELICE DE GIARDINI

1. Come, Thou al-might-y King, Help us Thy Name to sing, Help us to praise. Fa-ther all glo-ri-ous, O'er all vic-to-ri-ous, Come and reign o-ver us, An-cient of days.
2. Come, Thou In-car-nate Word, Gird on Thy might-y sword, Our pray'r at-tend. Come, and Thy peo-ple bless, And give Thy word suc-cess; Spir-it of ho-li-ness, On us de-scend.

223

Nobody Knows the Trouble I've Seen

SPIRITUAL

Refrain

No - bod - y knows the trou - ble I've seen,
No - bod - y knows my sor - row;
No - bod - y knows the trou - ble I've seen, Glo - ry hal - le - lu - jah!

Verse

1. Some - times I'm up, some - times I'm down,
2. Al - tho' you see me going 'long so,

Oh, yes, Lord! Some - times I'm al - most
Oh, yes, Lord! I have my trou - bles

D. C. al Fine

to the groun', Oh, yes, Lord!
here be - low, Oh, yes, Lord!

Classified Index

MAKING A LIVING

Farming
Ah, Lovely Meadows, 70
Choppin', 65
Cotton Song, The, 64
Desert Fruit, 8
Farmer, The, 181
Happy Plowman, The, 177
La Sandunga, 146
My Corn Seeds, 73
Peanut Picking Song, 68
Suzette, 23
Wheat Fields, 71

Herding and Cowboy
Buffalo Gals, 84
Cowboys' Christmas Ball, 85
Girl I Left Behind Me, The, 38
Great-Granddad, 115
Home on the Range, 82
Night Herding Song, 79
Old Chisholm Trail, 119
Old Texas, 78
Railroad Corral, 80
Shepherds Go with Their Flocks, 69

In the Forest
Ground Hog, 57
Lumberman's Alphabet, 50
Lumberman's Song, 52

Mining Songs
Down in a Coal Mine, 62
Mingo Mountain, 102
My Sweetheart's the Mule in the Mines, 63

On the Sea
Fishing Boats, 56
Sacramento, 105
Santy Anno, 104
Shenandoah, 109
Sponge Diver, The, 170
Suzette, 23
Whale, The, 58

Trade and Commerce
Bigerlow, 53
Connecticut Peddler, 30
Donkey Riding, 145
Erie Canal, 94
Hudson River Steamboat, 90
Push Boat, 89

Road and Railroad
Bullwhacker's Epic, 111
Don't Let Your Watch Run Down, 92
Drill, Ye Tarriers, 97
Driving Steel, 96
John Henry, 144
Mule Skinner Blues, 88
Sis Joe, 98
Teamster's Song, 18

Street Songs
Chairs to Mend, 28
Chimney Sweeper, 28
Grindstone Man, The, 46
Past Three O'Clock, 29
Tostadas, 190
Vendor's Song, 161

Work Rhythms
Choppin', 65
Don't Let Your Watch Run Down, 92
Driving Steel, 96
En Roulant Ma Boule, 20
Joe Magarac, 143
John Henry, 144
Mingo Mountain, 102
Railroad Cars Are Coming, The, 116
Santy Anno, 104
Shenandoah, 109
Sis Joe, 98

PLAYING INSTRUMENTS

Harmonic Instruments
AUTOHARP (throughout)
GUITAR
Dixie, 132
Mingo Mountain, 102
Paul Bunyan, 141
PIANO
A.D. 1620, 121
Cumberland Mountain Bear Chase, 54
Minuet Danced before George Washington, 36
Sleigh Ride, 206
PIANO CHORDING
Clementine, 107
Dixie, 132
O Susanna, 112
Sleigh Ride, 206
Turkey in the Straw, 93
TONE BARS
Brahms' Lullaby, 168
UKULELE
Aloha Oe, 152

Melody Instruments
Battle Hymn of the Republic, 134
Bugle Note, 7
Cumberland Mountain Bear Chase, 54
Fashions, 160
Golden Slumbers, 41
Grindstone Man, The, 46
Song of the Wind, 6
Sponge Diver, The, 170

Melody Instruments in Classroom Combination
America, 122
Hark! the Herald Angels Sing, 212
Home on the Range, 82
Marines' Hymn, 138
Santa Lucia, 164
Song of the Gypsy King, 198

Rhythm Instruments
BLOCKS—TONE AND SAND
Choppin', 65
Hudson River Steamboat, 90
DRUM
Bonita, 155
Deitch Company, 172
Desert Fruit, 8
Don't Let Your Watch Run Down, 92
Driving Steel, 96
Fingers of the Sun, 12
Johnny Comes Marching Home, 131
Pol Perica, 147
Rain Music, 201
Sambalele, 156
LATIN AMERICAN
Basay Down, 153
Fiesta, 188
Shy Incognita, 148
Teamster's Song, The, 18

SOCIAL LIVING

General
Cousin Jedediah, 32
Cumberland Mountain Bear Chase, 54
Feasting by the Ocean, 189
Mountain Trail, 10
Music in the Barn, 74
Navajo Happy Song, 191
Sing Everyone, 183

We're All Together Again, 157
Widdecombe Fair, 192
Wide Fields, The, 3

Conversational Songs
Cutting Bench, The, 44
Eight Bells, 106
Reuben and Rachel, 43
Santy Anno, 104
Shenandoah, 109
Shusti-Fidli, 173
Sis Joe, 98
Song of the Fishes, 108
We Three Kings, 210

Dance Songs
Buffalo Gals, 84
Dance Song, 149
Fiesta, 188
Mexican Hat Dance, 194
Music in the Barn, 74
Old Joe Clark, 61
Pol Perica, 147
Sambalele, 156
Shoot the Buffalo, 114
Sidewalks of New York, 158
Song of the Gypsy King, 198
Turkey in the Straw, 93
Weevily Wheat, 42
Zum Gali Gali, 169

Jokes and Nonsense
Abalone, 60
Baked Potato, 22
Basay Down, 153
Boll Weevil, 66
Bones, 184
Bonita, 155
Calaloo, 154
Clementine, 107
Eight Bells, 106
Lumberman's Song, 52
My Raincape, 19
Old Joe Clark, 61
Song of the Fishes, 108
Viva Panama, 150

Rounds
Bell, The, 13
Bells, 168
Chairs to Mend, 28
Christmas Is Coming, 209
Echo, 23
Ferry, The, 91
Hunting Song, 187
Moonlight, 15
Sing Everyone, 183
Sweep the Floor, 47
White Coral Bells, 214

226

SPECIAL SONGS FOR SPECIAL DAYS
Christmas
Christmas Is Coming, 209
Christmas Lullaby, 208
Hark! the Herald Angels Sing, 212
Shepherds, The, 208
Silent Night, 211
We Three Kings, 210

Patriotic
America, 122
America the Beautiful, 1
Dixie, 132
Star-Spangled Banner, The, 130

Purim
Purim Song, 214

Thanksgiving
Harvest Hymn, 204
Now Thank We All Our God, 205

Worship
Battle Hymn of the Republic, 134
Creation's Morning Song, 13
El Alabado, 16
New Created World, 215
O Morning Star, 48
Old Hundred, 25
Seasons, The, 202
PRIMITIVE BELIEF
Desert Fruit, 8
Fingers of the Sun, 12
Zuni Sunset Song, 14

SPECIAL SOURCES
Classic Composers
INSTRUMENTAL
A.D. 1620, 121
 MacDowell (*American*)
Carillon (L'Arlésienne Suite), 17
 Bizet (*French*)
Clair de Lune, 15
 Debussy (*French*)
Shepherd's Dance, 215
 German (*English*)
VOCAL
Brahms' Lullaby, 168
 Brahms (*German*)
Brook, The, 4
 Schubert (*German*)
Creation's Morning Song, 13
 Beethoven (*German*)

Hark! the Herald Angels Sing, 212
 Mendelssohn (*German*)
May, 216
 Mozart (*Austrian*)
New Created World, 215
 Haydn (*German*)
O Morning Star, 48
 Bach (*German*)
O Susanna, 112
 Foster (*American*)
Sacramento, 105
 Foster (*American*)

Contemporary Composers
INSTRUMENTAL
Grand Canyon Suite, The, 9
 Grofé (*American*)
On the Mall, 161
 Goldman (*American*)
VOCAL
Grindstone Man, The, 46
 Josef Marais (*American*)
Open Range, 2
 Milton Kaye (*American*)
Paul Bunyan, 141
 Dylan Todd (*American*)
Rain Music, 201
 Milton Kaye (*American*)
Seasons, The, 202
 Sibelius (*Finnish*)
Song of the Dawn, 86
 Milton Kaye (*American*)
Three Little Ships, 124
 Hoagy Carmichael (*American*)
Wheat Fields, 71
 Milton Kaye (*American*)

School Children
Cotton Song, The, 64
Rodeo Time, 193

Songs of American Indians
Desert Fruit, 8
 (*Papago*)
Fingers of the Sun, 12
 (*Yosemite*)
In the Sugar Camp, 49
 (*Ojibway*)
Lonely Is the Hogan, 207
 (*Navajo*)
My Corn Seeds, 73
 (*Papago*)
Navajo Happy Song, 191
 (*Navajo*)
Song of the Wind, 6
 (*Ute*)
Zuni Sunset Song, 14
 (*Zuni*)

Song Titles

Abalone	60
Ah, Lovely Meadows	70
Aloha Oe	152
America	122
America the Beautiful	1
American Hymn, The	219
A Pledge	222
A Song About a Day	222
At the Gate of Heaven	151
Baked Potato	22
Basay Down	153
Battle Hymn of the Republic	134
Beautiful Blue Danube, The	196
Bell, The	13
Bells	168
Bigerlow	53
Boll Weevil	66
Bones	184
Bonita	155
Brahms' Lullaby	168
Brook, The	4
Buffalo Gals	84
Bugle Note	7
Bullwhacker's Epic	111
Calaloo	154
Chairs to Mend	28
Chimney Sweeper	28
Choppin'	65
Christmas Is Coming	209
Christmas Lullaby	208
Clementine	107
Come, Thou Almighty King	223
Connecticut Peddler	30
Cotton Song, The	64
Cousin Jedediah	32
Cowboys' Christmas Ball	85
Creation's Morning Song	13
Cumberland Mountain Bear Chase	54
Cutting Bench, The	44
Dance Song	149
Deitch Company	172
Desert Fruit	8
Dixie	132
Donkey Riding	145
Don't Let Your Watch Run Down	92
Down in a Coal Mine	62
Down in the Valley	176
Drill, Ye Tarriers	97
Driving Steel	96
East, West—Home's Best	5
Echo	23
Eight Bells	106

El Alabado	16
En Roulant Ma Boule	20
Erie Canal	94
Farmer, The	181
Fashions	160
Feasting by the Ocean	189
Ferry, The	91
Fiesta	188
Fingers of the Sun	12
Finlandia	221
Fishing Boats	56
Girl I Left Behind Me, The	38
Golden Slumbers	41
Great-Granddad	115
Grindstone Man, The	46
Ground Hog	57
Happy Plowman, The	177
Hark! the Herald Angels Sing	212
Harvest Hymn	204
Home	217
Home on the Range	82
Hudson River Steamboat	90
Hunting Song	187
I Found a Horseshoe	174
In Good Old Colony Times	26
In the Sugar Camp	49
Jeanie with the Light Brown Hair	218
Joe Magarac	143
John Henry	144
Johnny Comes Marching Home	131
Johnny Has Gone for a Soldier	127
Jolly Miller	27
La Sandunga	146
Las Mañanitas	171
Lemon Tree, The	72
Little Burro	77
Little Old Sod Shanty, The	118
Lonely Is the Hogan	207
Lumberman's Alphabet	50
Lumberman's Song	52
Marines' Hymn	138
May	216
Mexican Hat Dance	194
Michie Banjo	166
Mingo Mountain	102
Mississippi Sounding Calls	103
Moonlight	15
Mountain Trail	10
Mule Skinner Blues	88
Music in the Barn	74

My Corn Seeds	73
My Raincape	19
My Sweetheart's the Mule in the Mines	63
Navajo Happy Song	191
New Created World	215
Night Herding Song	79
Nobody Knows the Trouble I've Seen	224
Now Thank We All Our God	205
O Morning Star	48
O Susanna	112
Old Chisholm Trail	119
Old Hundred	25
Old Joe Clark	61
Old Texas	78
Open Range	2
Our Kites Are Flying	162
Past Three O'Clock	29
Paul Bunyan	141
Peanut Picking Song	68
Pol Perica	147
Promised Land, The	110
Purim Song	214
Push Boat	89
Railroad Cars Are Coming, The	116
Railroad Corral	80
Rain Music	201
Reuben and Rachel	43
Riflemen of Bennington	128
Rodeo Time	193
Sacramento	105
Sambalele	156
Santa Lucia	164
Santy Anno	104
Seasons, The	202
Shenandoah	109
Shepherds, The	208
Shepherds Go with Their Flocks	69
Shoot the Buffalo	114
Shusti-Fidli	173
Shy Incognita	148
Sidewalks of New York	158
Silent Night	211
Sing Everyone	183
Sis Joe	98
Sleigh Ride	206
So Long	186
Soldier, Soldier	35
Song of the Dawn	86
Song of Destiny	200
Song of the Fishes	108
Song of the Gypsy King	198
Song of the Wind	6
Sponge Diver, The	170
Star-Spangled Banner, The	130
Stodola Pumpa	180
Suzette	23
Sweep the Floor	47
Teamster's Song, The	18
Tenting Tonight	136
Teru Teru Bozu	163
Three Little Ships	124
Tic-Tì, Tic-Tà	76
Tostadas	190
Turkey in the Straw	93
Under the Shady Trees	182
Utah Iron Horse	120
Vendor's Song	161
Viva Panama	150
Wabash Cannon Ball	100
Walking Song	185
We Three Kings	210
We're All Together Again	157
Wee Cooper of Fife	34
Weevily Wheat	42
Whale, The	58
Wheat Fields	71
White Coral Bells	214
Widdicombe Fair	192
Wide Fields, The	3
Woodman, Spare That Tree	178
Wraggle-Taggle Gypsies	40
Yankee Doodle	126
Zum Gali Gali	169
Zuni Sunset Song	14

Index to Instrumental Music

A.D. 1620	121
Carillon	17
Clair de Lune	15
Grand Canyon Suite, The	9
Minuet Danced before George Washington	36
On the Mall	161
Shepherd's Dance	215
Symphonic Themes	220

C⁸BAF   C⁰⁰⁸⁴ C⁻³ DB²AGA
B³CDBAG   MUCB   C D ECAG⁴ECDC
SPA¹¹⁵ FEDEDC (DBA:) DANIEL MY Bro
                      F²